# Underprivileged Overachiever

## A Crenshaw Story

by

Y. A. Salimu

TELEMACHUS PRESS

Publisher's Cataloging-In-Publication Data

Names: Salimu, Y. A. (Yohancé A.), author.
Title: Underprivileged overachiever : a Crenshaw story / by Y.A. Salimu.
Description: Dublin, Ohio : Telemachus Press, [2020] | Includes index. | Interest age level: 014-018. |
    Summary: The true story of an African American man who grew up amid poverty, homelessness,
    gang violence and drugs. But unlike many others, he found success. He reached for the skies and
    became a multi-decorated graduate of the Air Force Academy.
Identifiers: ISBN 9781951744328 (paperback) | ISBN 9781951744335 (hardback) | ISBN
    9781951744311 (ebook)
Subjects: LCSH: Salimu, Y. A. (Yohancé A.) | Homeless youth--California--Los Angeles--Biography. |
    African American military cadets--California--Los Angeles--Biography. | Crenshaw High School
    (Los Angeles, Calif.)--Students--Biography. | Brothers--California--Los Angeles. | FIRST
    Robotics Competition (2009) | Success. | CYAC: Salimu, Y. A. (Yohancé A.) | Homeless youth--
    California--Los Angeles--Biography. | African American military cadets--California--Los Angeles--
    Biography. | Crenshaw High School (Los Angeles, Calif.)--Students--Biography. | Brothers--
    California--Los Angeles. | FIRST Robotics Competition (2009) | Success. | LCGFT:
    Autobiographies. | BISAC: YOUNG ADULT NONFICTION / Biography & Autobiography /
    General.
Classification: LCC E185.97.S24 A3 2020 (print) | LCC E185.97.S24 (ebook) | DDC
979.49400496073092 B--dc23

**Underprivileged Overachiever: A Crenshaw Story**

The publisher does not have any control over and does not assume any responsibility for author or third-party websites or their content.

Cover designed by Kendra Cagle https://www.5lakesdesign.com/

Cover art:
Copyright © Depositphotos/35619895/Los Angeles downtown skyline at sunset – Photo by dell640
Depositphotos/45087579/Grey concrete texture wall, bright white background-wallpapers: bright for walls – Photo by leszekglasner
Depositphotos/274654378/Cheerful young graduated student man isolated – Photo by tomwang
Shutterstock/ 422931823/autumn, childhood, dream, leisure and people concept - happy little boy playing with wooden toy plane outdoors – Photo by chuanpis
Shutterstock/306992957/Unknown male person silhouette. Back lit studio isolated – Photo by Evdokimov Maxim
Shutterstock/1152353915 Fighter jets doing demonstrations at one air show organized by international airport from Timisoara. Sunset time – Photo by Loan Florin Cnejevici

Unless otherwise noted, the images in this book are used with permission from Robert S. Helfman (The Shawdog).

Published by Telemachus Press, LLC
7652 Sawmill Road
Suite 304
Dublin, Ohio 43016
http://www.telemachuspress.com

Visit the author website:
http://www.YASalimu.com

ISBN: 978-1-951744-31-1 (eBook)
ISBN: 978-1-951744-32-8 (paperback)
ISBN: 978-1-951744-33-5 (hardback)

Library of Congress Control Number: 2020916454

Category: **YOUNG ADULT NONFICTION** / Biography & Autobiography / General

Version 2020.08.28

# Praise

OMG. That was my reaction after reading the words and understanding the hardships endured and overcome in Underprivileged Overachiever: A Crenshaw Story. For all the stereotypes of growing up in South Los Angeles, this is a no-holds-barred story how a teenager somehow made it to the Air Force Academy while being homeless and facing obstacle after obstacle.

It's stunning for its truth and refusal to hold anything back. I'm not a big fan of profanity but understand how it's used in sports and in life and used in telling this story. I was an outsider and observer during Yohancé Salimu's Crenshaw football days. He played on one of the most talented Crenshaw teams ever with the likes of future NFL players De'Anthony Thomas and Hayes Pullard. As a sportswriter for the Los Angeles Times, looking back it was his story of perseverance that should have risen to the top.

Fortunately, we all now get to look back and understand the depths of despair that he was able to overcome and the many kind people he ran into that helped him along the way. Some of those same people, like his football coach, Robert Garrett, are still trying to help others in a world that's changing but also not changing.

This story is shocking for its honesty. It might need a warning label before parents allow their teenagers to read. But it's a compelling read and one that provides insights into today's daily struggles for families seeking a path to a better life.

—Eric Sondheimer
Los Angeles Times

This is not a Horatio Alger story. It's better, more honest. When you're done reading it, you might have some questions. First, you might question whether you should have complained as much as you complained about most of the things you complained about. The answer to that question is probably no. Second, you'll wonder whether you could have achieved what Yohancé achieved had you inherited and been forced to endure his circumstances. The answer to that question is almost certainly no. Third, you might wonder whether you know anyone else who is tougher and braver and smarter and more indomitable than Yohancé. The answer to that question is the easiest one. It is irrefutably no.

—Edward C. Hopkins Jr.
Attorney, Essayist & U.S. Air Force Academy Class of 1995

"I'm in love with this story and this author! Yohancé tore his heart open and poured out a soulful story of fear, love, rage and redemption. This is not just a coming of age story, this is x-ray vision into the mind of a boy forced to grow up too fast and build a life with scraps to feed his imagination. By discovering his superpower and his kryptonite were one and the same, Yohancé learned how to craft his own future with an iron will and hard-to-swallow ego. Yet no matter what, he kept going. If you mentor young men, this story will help you redouble your efforts to keep reaching into the darkest wells to raise up refreshing talent like this. This compelling story can't be read on a diet, you binge, hard … and you don't stop until that last page turns. I wish more young men were brave enough to bare their lives so freely, our society needs this so much more than we know!"

—Emille Bryant,
Author of *Start With A Sparkle*

"Yohancé's manuscript is evocative. Period. Point blank. Full stop. In this world of distractions, take an entire day to read this book—straight through. Yohancé will masterfully paint a picture on the canvas of your mind and naked soul. While the emotional journey includes some sobering realities,

Yohancé also invites you to embrace wonderful glimpses of resilience, courage, and triumph.

The vivid language in each chapter paints a picture of scenes alien to most and indescribable to all void of the SH!T it takes to be a real man. When you recover from the emotional shock of this story, you may draw your own conclusions about food insecurity, homelessness, sexual violence, and rites of passage to greatness.

A chance meeting with Dwayne "The Rock" Johnson, the larger-than-life wrestler and big-screen movie star, imbued in Yohancé the attitude to keep reaching for a brighter tomorrow. In a world where celebrity voices seldom have the wisdom we desire, The Rock said the right thing at the right time to the right person."

—Rauhmel Fox, Director and CEO
AFA GRAD INC.
http://www.afagrad.com
"Be an example in your duty and in private life."


"Yohancé Salimu has endured more obstacles, setbacks, fear and struggle in his youth than most will face in a lifetime. The story and writing are as gritty and in-your-face as the streets he came up in and immerses the reader into a tense, chaotic world where the wrong move can get you killed. He achieves what would seem unachievable through grit and ambition but also with the panache of a street performer, where you're amazed, heartbroken and at times laughing out loud, at his surreal journey. Throughout the book, Yohancé is hungry—literally—as food was always scarce and there was never enough to satisfy. You can feel his deep, driving hunger not only for food, but to matter, to feel "normal", accepted, successful and worthy—a struggle all of us can relate to at times. This story is powerful in its message, unforgettable in its telling—and needed in the world right now."

—D.J. Eagle Bear Vanas,
Author of *The Tiny Warrior: A Path to Personal Discovery & Achievement*

# A Note from the Author

Geospatial Q & A Inc. is a Delaware Charitable Nonstock Exempt Corporation. Formally recognized by the IRS as a 501(c)(3) specifically a 509(a)(2) under IRC.

Geospatial Q & A Inc.'s activities & exempt purposes include:

Scientific
- Research Institutes & Public Policy Analysis
- Conduct research and/or public policy analysis

Educational
- Provide educational programs within the formal educational system or offered as an adjunct to the traditional school curriculum which help students succeed in school and prepare for life.
- Broker resources for the benefit of local schools.

Charitable
- Community & Neighborhood Development
- Focus broadly on strengthening, unifying and building the economic, cultural, educational and social services of an urban community or neighborhood.

At Geospatial Q & A Inc. our goal is to be the strongest and most impactful charitable organization this world has ever seen. The publishing of this book is part of this effort.

While the original story remains the creation of our President and CEO, Yohancé Salimu, all proceeds from *Underprivilege Overachiever–A Crenshaw Story*, shall be owned and hence collected by Geospatial Q & A Inc. To put it plainly, and in the words of our leader, "Every penny this book generates will go directly towards creating opportunities for underprivileged youth. Period!"

Geospatial Q & A Inc. is enrolled in the PayPal Giving Fund to receive qualified sponsorship payments and unrestricted donations.
To contribute, visit https://www.paypal.com/fundraiser/charity/3995143

You may also do as the cool kids do and use the QR Code here:

# Disclaimer

The Internal Revenue Code (IRC) Section 513(i) defines a "qualified sponsorship payment" as any payment made by any person engaged in a trade or business with respect to which there is no arrangement or expectation that such person will receive any substantial return benefit other than the use or acknowledgement of the name or logo (or product lines) of such person's trade or business in connection with the activities of the Geospatial Q & A Inc. that receives such payment.

# Purpose

The primary reason I wrote this book is to tell my story to those that need to hear it.

I'm not a writer; I'm a storyteller, and this is my unapologetic attempt at putting it all down on paper.

I know there are certain people that really need this book, and I know it took me a while, but I have finally written it … just for you.

# Where I'm From

I'm from Nothing, No how, and No way
From that ruthless Dog eat dog type of shady play

GIMMIE THAT!

Still alive 'cause these food stamps that put a lil grub on my tray

I'm from that rock bottom starting place
The one man assumed to finish last in this race

I'm from those broken shelters that call themselves a home
Knocking on God's door 'cause I don't wanna walk this path alone

I'm from NOTHING, No how, and No way
But every morning I wake up, and pray I see a better day

Y.A. Salimu

# Preface

My name is Yohancé.

Rhymes with Beyoncé, starts with a Y. YOH-HON-SAY.

I'm smart, I'm intelligent, and I'm extremely good-looking.

If I did not think so highly of myself, why would I write a memoir?

OK—my biggest flaw is my excessive ego. But it may be the reason I have made it this far in life.

I feel the key to success is perspective, which is why most of the time I see the glass as half full.

I also think I am funny. Look, I'll prove this one to you.

> *Why did the lady chicken cross the road?*
> *'Cause those guys across the street kept trying to offer her their cocks!*

Sometimes my jokes fail. Sometimes my good looks fail. Sometimes my smarts, my wits, and all my grand abilities fail. But what never fails is my ego. I truly believe when it comes to living life ... I got this shit.

Also ...

I don't have good boundaries, which many of my friends will tell you. I frequently invade their space to give them bear hugs to show 'em I really care about 'em.

I am loud, affectionate, and the very opposite of a private person. I'll tell you just about anything about me if you ask. And while you never asked me to write this book, it's the only way for me to truly show you who I am and where I'm from.

Just a bit more before we get started …

I acknowledge that I am a mere pawn and that the only one playing 4-D chess is God. I also acknowledge that a lot of what I am about to show you in this book is VERY embarrassing, which is why I need to tell you the most embarrassing thing in my life first.

One day, my mother overheard my phone conversation with a girl-friend. I was talking about not caring that my girlfriend was on her period and telling her we could still have sex. My mother overheard every detail. Later she told me it was not smart to have that conversation in the same small room that your mom, little brother, and you all sleep in—at a homeless shelter.

Now that you know this about me, nothing else I tell you in this book can embarrass me.

# Table of Contents

## Section 1 / First Quarter

## Section 2 / Second Quarter

# Half-Time

# Section 3 / Third Quarter

# Section 4 / Fourth Quarter

# Underprivileged Overachiever

## A Crenshaw Story

# Section 1 / First Quarter

Looking forward to the journey

*Like I said in the preface ... I got this shit!*

# Chapter 1
## Starting at Rock Bottom

*—He said the right thing, at the right time,
to the right person*

NO ONE EVER wants to wake up like this, I thought to myself. Pots
and pans were banging together in the kitchen. I could hear the commotion
even though I had stuffed my ears with the last few pieces of toilet paper in
the house.

My mother, Tabia Salimu, was dancing in the kitchen, banging the pots
like drums. She was not cooking. There had been no food for weeks. She was
trying to wake her two sons who, if she let them, would sleep through their
whole summer vacation.

We'd sleep for as long as we could if it meant we could escape our
hunger, our tears, or our mother's next episode. That's what my little brother
Kumasi and I called our mom's bipolar and psychotic breaks from reality:
episodes.

It was late August in 2006, and I had very little motivation to get up.
Kumasi rolled out of bed first, but I was the older brother, so I leapt from
bed and burst into the bathroom before him.

"Know why I get to pee first?" I asked Kumasi.

"I don't care, just hurry up," he retorted.

"It's because I'm the leader," I said triumphantly.

Kumasi was eleven years old. Two years his senior, I was the man of the house. I told the boy to wash his face and brush his teeth—to follow my example. I would never mislead him. We got dressed in the same clothes we had worn the day before, and marched toward the kitchen to greet our mother.

When we entered the kitchen, we found that our mother had been banging on the pots with a pair of big wooden spoons as she danced to her own tune. Kumasi and I yelled, "Good morning!" to take our mom's attention off her stellar performance. She stopped banging the pots, snapped back into reality, and greeted us back, "Good morning, my loves." I had already decided that today my mother's mental health was not going to make me sad. Today was going to be a happy day, though I still had to poke the bear.

"Mom, since we are not American Indians, and that performance of yours wasn't a rain dance, I was just wondering: Was this some new ritual you discovered to put food on the table?"

She laughed at my joke, which was a relief, because she didn't always find me funny. People in our type of situation had to find a way to laugh at themselves from time to time. Mom replied defiantly, "No, I am not an American Indian. I am a North American-born African of Cuban descent. And if you so please, you may call this performance the Food Dance."

She smiled warmly at me and Kumasi as she glided down the kitchen floor and kissed us both on the mouth. In small doses, she could be a very sweet woman and one of my favorite people in the world.

"Can this pregnant lady get fed anytime soon today?" she asked the two of us as she pointed to her small tummy.

"Mom, are you really pregnant again?" Kumasi asked with despair in his voice.

"Boy, be quiet … I ask the questions around here," I jokingly told my little brother. "Mom, when were you going to tell us the news, so that we could start prioritizing you eating first?"

"I just found out today," she exclaimed as she pushed past us to grab car keys from the table. "It's almost noon. Are you two ready to go to the park?"

We had slept in that morning and almost missed the highlight of the whole summer. Dwayne "The Rock" Johnson was coming to the hood to screen his new movie, *Gridiron Gang*.

My mom drove us all to the park in the purple Toyota hatchback. The car had been donated to us by Alexandria House, an amazing women's charity in Los Angeles. We had just gotten this car, and it was the only thing we owned that could fool outsiders into thinking our family lived an average life. Feeding our bellies was always a priority over feeding the gas tank, so we rarely drove anywhere. We mostly took public transportation with bus tokens provided by the city. Today was different, though. We had been looking forward to this special day for weeks.

When we arrived at the park, we immediately began to scan the crowd to find The Rock. My mom was the first to give up; she glided over to the swing sets where she began to wind up her swing like a kid and spin in circles. Kumasi and I did more searching, but finally discovered The Rock was not here yet.

I spotted a lady in a suit talking on the phone, looking frustrated and very busy. A few of the younger boys walked up to her and asked if The Rock was really coming. She smiled and said, "Certainly, he is, young man. He would never disappoint his fans." I wanted to believe her, but I had my doubts; on the drive over, I told Kumasi that the chance of The Rock showing up to this event was slim to none.

The Rock's new movie, *Gridiron Gang*, was about helping inner city boys like us, but I felt showing up in person was not worth it to him. He wants to make money, sell tickets, and play the "I care" card as long as it is lucrative for him. But me, I lived in a dog-eat-dog world where I had no time for someone who wasn't real, who wasn't walking the walk.

"OK, Kumasi, let me break this shit down for a niglet (I had a bunch of nicknames for Kumasi, but niglet was always my favorite). That big-ass nigga The Rock ain't comin' today, tomorrow, or no damn time in the future. He ain't tryna see our black asses, and tha's just real-talk. Black people dodge bullets, we don't run toward 'em. So ain't no way this nigga 'bout ta show up in the hood. I cain't see him coming to Athens Park to show us this new movie for free, anyhow. The shit ain't even in theaters yet, niglet! This whole thing fake as hell!"

My little speech had gotten louder, drawing a crowd of boys to form around us.

"I just wanna see the movie," Kumasi said. "If he actually shows up, then that's just a bonus for me."

That dog-eat-dog mentality had been hammered into me a long time ago. So long ago that it felt like a different lifetime. Back when we were much younger, living homeless in downtown Los Angeles with my mom, we did anything to survive. That was back in the year 2000, when the core gang of five was together (my mom and her five kids at the time). I was seven years old. My four siblings and I would bounce around from shelter to shelter on Skid Row, doing a million things that kids aged five to twelve should not do. Skid Row is the homeless capital of the world, a shithole of a place, or "community," located in the heart of downtown Los Angeles. The amount of lawlessness, drug infestation, and hopelessness in this area is legendary. Gangs, drugs, violence, those were just normal parts of my life, though I had somehow escaped the worst of it.

My mother had escaped Skid Row after years of repeated bouts with homelessness and moved us into an apartment in the hood; it was a small but significant upgrade. That change of environment allowed me to quit doing drugs, stop fighting in the streets, and find better male role models to look up to. Hanging around to meet The Rock was one of those opportunities.

Most of the times I was doing drugs it was with my mom, so her making a change meant we all had to make changes. There were certainly no guarantees as to where my life was headed, but seeing my childhood hero sure couldn't hurt. That's a big reason why we were at that park that day. We needed more motivation—a reason to keep going.

But I worried that my little brother would get his hopes up too much, and the disappointment of not getting to meet The Rock could crush him. While he pretended he did not really care one way or the other, I could see right through him. Kumasi had been looking forward to this for weeks, and it was one of the only things he could be happy about. Life was hard, and my family was struggling. Our father was *sort of* in the picture, but the five kids he had given my mother were not doing as well as the other ten whose moms were a little more stable. My father, Abidala Salimu, was more of a lifeline than a provider. He would show up if we really needed him, but for the most part, my mother and her five children struggled together.

Around 2004, my mother became increasingly mentally unstable; taking care of us and herself at the same time was becoming impossible. My other siblings had started to flee my mother's household to move in with friends. Over a period of less than a year, three of them had moved out, even though all of them were still minors. It was the summer of 2005 when my older siblings fully understood the situation: my mom was not working, she was unable to feed us, and bills were piling up on the table. But being the two youngest children, my little brother and I just stayed put and suffered alongside her.

We weren't just at this park to meet The Rock. School was out for the summer, and until I started the eighth grade in a few weeks, I had no free school lunch to look forward to. We heard there would be food served, and it would surely be the only meal my family ate that day.


The Rock's nickname was The People's Champion. All of his wrestling moves were named in that spirit. He would drop his elbow on you and end your whole career—that was the people's elbow. The Rock would lift one eyebrow and look daringly at someone—the people's eyebrow. He had a bunch of catchphrases. The rest of the kids in the park were running around doing wrestling moves and pretending to be the people's champion.

His most famous catchphrase involved asking the crowd if they could smell what The Rock was cooking. People loved repeating it. Every few seconds someone was yelling at the top of their lungs, asking if everyone in the park could smell what The Rock was cooking. Of course I could smell it. I was eating my third plate of food. But then I heard my little brother's voice. The boy almost made me drop my chicken.

"IF YOU SMELLALALALAL!

WHAT THE ROCK!

IS COOKING!"

Kumasi yelled it so loudly that everyone's head turned. Best of all, The Rock was standing a few feet away in the parking lot. The World Wrestling Entertainment superstar approached the crowd with energy and intensity. He electrified the whole crowd with a smile and the people's eyebrow. The smallest kids ran up to climb all over him. His muscles seemed bigger in person, especially as he began to curl several boys with one arm. The whole gathering must have consisted of less than a hundred people, so we were all super close to him when we took our seats to hear him speak.

The Rock's speech was about what we meant to him. He told the crowd that communities like ours are near and dear to his heart, and that he made this movie to inspire more young men and women to make the right choices. I believed him. When he ended his speech and started to screen *Gridiron Gang* for us, I knew in my heart that this day would be one of the most influential days of my life.

The movie showed a group of boys united on the football field with the same goal—to win. I could be something like them and join a different type of gang—a gridiron gang. The encouraging speeches that The Rock gave in the movie were powerful, but his words to us in the park that day were even more so.

I will always remember when he looked me right in the eye and said, "Drugs, gangs, and this cycle of violence is not your only option. And I believe in you, and in your success."

I really needed to hear The Rock say that, because I was starting to get tired of watching my mom and little brother suffer. And I needed to know that I could help change that.

# Chapter 2
# Hunger for Strength

SHARING ALWAYS CAME easier to Kumasi and me because we grew up in a household where the two of us had to split the crumbs. Being the smallest two children in the house made us vulnerable when it came to staking a claim for what was ours. There was a finite amount of resources. If we were not on guard, we could lose anything to the faster hands of our older siblings.

I always ate with my arms on the table to help me react faster to a sista stealing my cornbread—or a brotha choosing my plate to take seconds from. It didn't stop at food either. If I managed to save a dresser drawer full of coins I found off the street, they could quickly turn up missing. This fierce competition for survival only eased up when my older siblings moved. Now it was time for me as the new man of the house to start making some changes—until my brother Abasi came back, that is.

Abasi decided to come back for a short stint to live with Kumasi, my mom, and me in the summer of 2006. He was the sibling I least wanted to compete against for my survival. He was sixteen at the time, and three years my senior. The age difference may seem small, but Abasi had gone through several transformations over the last few years. Puberty had turned him into a giant, as he'd nearly grown a whole foot taller and was developing muscles I had never seen on humans before. He was a ravenous eater; he would sit down with us to eat—and then eat the second dinner he brought for himself. (He called our meager meal his appetizer.)

Abasi funded his insatiable appetite with a few small-time illegal hustles. Abasi was the first *businessman* I had ever seen rob his suppliers and his customers at the same time. He would acquire a certain type of *merchandise*, sell it, and then steal it back from his customers. Back in those days I thought to myself, if I just stayed out of his way, I might survive long enough to go to the same high school as him—Crenshaw High. Everyone knew he was a dangerous man, both on and off the football field.

According to Abasi, there were bigger threats in South Central Los Angeles than him. I just couldn't see exactly how, since at six-foot-six he towered over most grown men and was built like a house. He was also the most aggressive person I'd ever met. He never stopped stealing food from my plate, grabbing it quickly while I was watching the news on our six-inch TV. When I turned back to my plate, half of my mashed potatoes would be gone. Then Abasi would point at Kumasi, which confused me. Did he believe I could be fooled into thinking Kumasi had stolen food from me, or was he telling me that now I could take from Kumasi's plate? Either way, I refused his gesture. Most nights that this happened, I would throw the first punch. I loathed getting beat up by Abasi, but I'd learned a long time ago that I would have to fight for everything I got.

Eventually Abasi had taken enough money from people to buy his own set of weights for a small home gym. He wanted my help unboxing the whole thing and tightening all the screws. I told him I would help only if he taught me how to lift weights. I wanted to get big and strong enough to knock Abasi the fuck out. I was tired of watching my brother continue to get bigger and bigger, while I shrunk twice a day; first outwardly, and then again in my spirit.

The weight on the bar never was adjusted for me. If I couldn't lift the same weight as my big brother, then I couldn't work out with him. He would not waste time putting what he called "bitch weight" on the bar for me. I was forced to keep up, and eventually I developed a few muscles of my own. The free weight training lessons soon came to an end; Abasi decided that he had more than paid his debt back to me. "From now on, you cain't touch ma shit unless you pay me, *Yohancé*," Abasi told me. He called me by my first name instead of my middle name, Ajamu. It always felt awkward and teasing whenever my family called me by my first name because there was an unwritten rule that we never did that to each other. Family calls you by your middle name.

The main reason being called my first name by my family members was such an insult was because it was like they were calling me someone else's name. They didn't know Yohancé. They only knew Ajamu. Yohancé is a well-mannered, intelligent boy who speaks proper English and makes his teachers proud. Ajamu is a mean, foulmouthed hood nigga that throws the first punch and don't take shit from nobody. So in calling me by my first name, Abasi was essentially calling me a bitch and telling me to act accordingly.

I do love both of my names, but family calls me by my middle name. Only.

"*Yohancé*, do you understand our new agreement?" Abasi even spoke to me using proper English, which was so very alien to hear at home. At home we spoke comfortably in a slang that came naturally. We didn't pronounce every syllable of every word unless we were at school. Basically, he was trying to get under my skin.

Abasi now wanted me to start paying him for weightlifting—but what currency did he think I had? Food was the only currency I could provide. I would now eat only half of my dinner in order to pay Abasi to use his gym. He would sometimes accept food I brought home from the free lunches at school. Most of the time he would call those meals a donation toward his NFL career. He would say I needed to give more food in order to lift weights. Eventually I became frustrated by this stupid bartering system.

By lifting weights, I was getting stronger. But by not eating my entire meals, I was getting smaller. Was I training myself to win a fight against Abasi, or was I risking the chance of getting beaten up even worse? One day I got brave and asked my brother a question. "Why do you still want me to pay you when you have all this money and are buying all these nice clothes and shit now?"

Abasi had a quick answer: "Don't you worry about what I got." He told me that if I needed new clothes, I could take his old hand-me-downs that he had thrown into the corner. I pushed back, telling him I didn't care about his clothes; I was tired of giving him my food! I was tired of paying to use a gym that he wasn't even using much anymore! "*It's not fair!*" I was yelling by now.

My brother started to smile at me sadistically when he heard my rant. "Fuck outta here with that fair bullshit. Ain't nuthin' fair in this life, and yo bitch ass needs to grow up and stop whining about yo fuckin' problems. You lucky I even let you use my shit this long. I'm 'bouta stop doin' favors for yo ungrateful ass. Everything you wearin' right now is my shit that I done gave you; even them drawls, nigga! You wouldn't even have no underwear on if it wasn't for me, bitch! I don't owe you shit!"

The lump in my throat felt real heavy, but I had to be tough. I knew a fight was coming. I wasn't going to let him break me down and kick my ass at the same time. I told him I was going to stop paying him and start sneaking into his room when he was not home. He threw the first punch that day. But for the first time in my life, I thought I could win.

Abasi punched me square in the stomach. He expected me to fall and the fight to be instantly over. Instead of having the wind knocked out of me, I found that my abdominal muscles could now take his punch. I surprised Abasi with a quick two-punch combo to the jaw, which I had to leap into the air to deliver. I chopped that giant down with that two-piece combo, and upon landing on my feet, I realized that I was too close to him. As he swung his fist to bash my head in, I rapidly retreated and narrowly escaped. The giant had fallen over from missing his powerful swing, and I knew I had to strike once more in order to claim my victory. I sprinted back to Abasi, advancing faster than I had ever moved before. He reached to pull me down to the ground with him, but I grabbed hold first. I reached my hands deep into his long afro and grabbed the roots to this man's soul. When I felt I had a firm enough grasp, I began backpedaling through the house. Out of the bedroom, down the hallway, and in a circle in the living room, I dragged Abasi by his afro until two dark puffs of hair separated from his scalp. When the battle was over, I feared for my life and sprinted out the front door of our apartment. I had won that fight. And as I walked down the street toward a friend's house, I tossed around the two little hairy trophies that I had to prove it.

# Chapter 3
## Painting the Jungles

AFTER BEATING UP Abasi, I walked around my neighborhood for a few hours to reflect on the can of whoop-ass I had just opened. The summer night was warm, and it wasn't too late to take an evening stroll in the Jungles. This neighborhood was beautiful. It was full of tall banana trees and palm trees, and had winding roads that climbed up a steep hill to converge at a massive park in the middle of the community—Jim Gilliam Park.

There were no houses in the Jungles, just row after row of large apartment buildings. This tight-knit community never felt dangerous to me, despite what the news warned us. People who really knew this area always put an "s" on the end of our name for the area. They knew that there were multiple layers to "the Jungle," and thus labeled it "the Jungles."

### Meeting The Gangbangers

The Jungles was run by a Blood Gang. Before I knew them, these scary-looking guys hanging around—patrolling—the neighborhood were my biggest obstacle. I'd avoid any part of the park or neighborhood if I saw them. The Jungles is a pretty big place, and though there are a lot of Bloods everywhere, it is still possible to avoid them, just not forever.

I had my first encounter with the Bloods in the summer of 2006. I was walking in the park right after sunset. An ice cream truck had been rolling through the neighborhood, and the Bloods called to me as I was walking the winding path in the park with my head down.

"Aye, lil nigga!"

"Come here!"

They were standing about 200 feet ahead at the ice cream truck. I could have run away, but I was just too sad. My mom had just had another episode of loud and crazy yelling at me. She'd chased me around the apartment chastising me for asking her what was for dinner. Had I asked her the wrong way or been impolite? Had I sounded entitled or spoiled because I had already started to get accustomed to eating every night? It had been two weeks of having dinner every night, and perhaps I had begun to count on it. Nonetheless, I was too demoralized after running out of the apartment to run away from these gangbangers. I walked right on up to the ice cream truck.

"Get you something," one of the three Bloods told me as he pointed at the ice cream truck. I don't know if he could see the dried tears or the utter despair on my face as I lifted my head to meet his gaze. It was getting dark, and it took everything I had left in me to clear the lump in my throat and answer him.

"I ain't got no money."

The three gang members exploded into laughter as they looked me up and down. They began taking turns roasting me.

"You think we thought—YOU—had money!?"

"Look at those shoes! Your socks aren't just busted out the front of 'em, you actually getting traction like the Flintstones!"

"Boy what's up with yo shirt!? You look like you get all yo nutrition from sucking on the collar of that raggedy thing!"

"If you get one more hole in those jeans you gon' be wearin' shorts, young man!"

"If anyone ever needs a dollar from you, hell will have frozen over!"

They were an animated and energetic group that made me smile and laugh at myself. I told them what happened at my home, and they bought me an ice cream. They empathized with me and said stuff like, "That shit happens in the hood," and they gave me a few dollars to go buy dinner for my mom and little brother. After that I saw these guys almost every week just hanging around my neighborhood. And even though I wasn't a Blood, I felt a connection to 'em.

## Making Friends in the Jungles

The Jungles was my home, and I knew almost every street in it, because I made new friends there daily. Boys and girls of all ages would come up to the park to play together. Basketball, football, tennis ... Jim Gillian had it all. The park even had a putting green for golf. My apartment building was at the top of the hill in the Jungles; a hop, jump, and a skip away from the basketball courts. I could walk out onto the balcony of my apartment building and see who was playing basketball. If I saw someone I could play ball with, I laced up my shoes and ran outside to go make a new friend.

In the summer, basketball continued all day and night in the Jungles. The lights would come on when the sun went down, but they would never turn off like they did in most parks in the city when it got too late. Some of the coolest friends I met at the park would only show up after midnight. I'd peek around my balcony at the court in the middle of the night and see two or three boys shooting a basketball. If the people on the court were much older than me, or looked like gangbangers, I would not go outside. If the group looked two or three people short of a pick-up game, then I would ask my brothers to come outside with me. If my brothers said no, then I would knock on doors in our apartment building to get friends to sneak out to play ball with me.

Making friends on the basketball court had to be the easiest thing I had ever done in my life. I didn't even have to speak. Walking across the small alley of a street and standing on the basketball court was all I had to do to get placed into a game. Once my team won, they would turn their heads around to look at me with a puzzling smile.

"Who are you?" one of the boys asked me.

"My name is Yohancé. Rhymes with Beyoncé, starts with a Y. YOH-HON-SAY," I told him.

"Well my name is Tarrell, Yohancé. I think it's cool that you got one of those African names. Is you African?" he asked me.

"No. I'm black, just like you, but my father gave all of his children African names."

"Man, that's powerful! Does your name have some sort of meaning?"

"Yeah, it means God's gift," I said.

"With a name like that, you must be the most arrogant man I have ever met. You were good in that last game, but I wouldn't exactly say you were 'God's gift' to basketball."

Tarrell made me laugh and was one of the few people that I felt I could be 100 percent myself with from day one. Because the two of us were the same age, we had seen each other in passing at Audubon Middle School before. We became really close friends. After any turmoil I experienced at home, I usually spent the night at his house.

Since I had just beat up my big brother Abasi, I walked the five blocks through the Jungles for refuge at Tarrell's apartment.


Tarrell had shown me months ago how to break into his apartment complex, but somehow I had forgotten how. All of these large buildings had their own separate security systems, but they also usually had a secret passage into the complex. Some buildings had extensive underground passages, while others had large trees you could climb and then simply hop over onto a communal balcony. I knew Tarrell's building had one of the five or so locked doors that were actually broken. Which locked door I had to shake open was what I could not remember.

Eventually I ninja'd my way into the building, where I whispered Tarrell's name outside of his door. His mom and dad were good people who usually let me stay the night. And I definitely needed to stay, or I faced a second round of fighting Abasi, so I asked Tarrell to sneak me into the house. If he could just put me in a closet for a few hours of sleep, I knew I would survive to tell the tale.

When Tarrell's father opened the closet door the next morning, he smiled and handed me a plate of scrambled eggs and toast. Apparently Tarrell had spilled the beans the night before. Mr. Smith was an understanding man. After his son explained my whole situation to him, Mr. Smith made up his mind how he would help me.

"Yohancé, I'm going to teach you how to lay the smackdown," Mr. Smith said.

I thought I had misheard him. Mr. Smith, a big, powerful black man, was offering to teach me how to fight. There was no way I would turn down his offer.


Mr. Smith took his son and me to a real gym a few times over the next few days and showed us how to lift weights and fight. Tarrell and I sparred as his father taught us how to properly throw a punch and how to fight standing up or on the ground. He wore us out. He introduced us to a mixture of martial arts that he told us to only use in self-defense. I played with the idea of using some of the bone-breaking techniques on Abasi, but I understood how serious Mr. Smith was about his warning. I stayed with the Smith family for a few days before I was ready to go back home. When I returned, Abasi was gone.

# Chapter 4
## Who's Gonna Win This Fight?

**Strong Leadership / Wrong Direction**

I WAS TOO busy trying to survive to fully understand the growing racial tension between my peers at Audubon Middle School. Half of my time was spent searching for or eating a free school lunch, while the other half was spent studying in my classrooms. Even after the bell rang for a short break, I would not leave my instructor's classrooms until I had mastered the lesson for the day. I knew education would be my golden ticket out of pain and misery, and I was laser-eye focused on my prize, so much so that I did not see the pending threat creeping up on me.

Audubon had a sixty-forty student population of black and Hispanic. We were known for being a bad or "hood" school that you only sent your kid to if you could not afford private school. Since no one from the hood could afford to escape the hood, we were all stuck at Audubon together.

Unlike most of the kids in middle school, I would show up very early to school, way before the class bell would ring. The saying "The early bird gets the worm" could not have been more true at my school, because there was more food to be had first thing in the morning. I would get to the cafeteria early and come away with several breakfast burritos, orange juice boxes, and a pocket full of snacks. There was so little that could have made me any happier.

One morning, after getting a good haul of cafeteria food, I strolled over to the basketball courts. I met up with my buddies Tarrell Smith and Jarell Hill. Just then we noticed two boys getting aggressive over a dispute about money. There were seldom enough people to play a full five-on-five basketball game at this early hour, so players would settle for playing a different game called shooting for bucks. Both players would stand on opposite sides of a basketball hoop and shoot three-point shots one after the other. The first player to make seven shots won the game and took a small amount of money from the loser's pocket.

Jarrell, Tarrell, and I watched this dispute between the two, one black and one Hispanic, escalate. Suddenly, I decided to step in. But instead of playing peacemaker, I suggested these kids fight; I've always enjoyed a good fight.

I spread the word quickly, and within minutes there were about a hundred kids on the blacktop playground. I ordered them to circle around my two contestants. Jarrell and Tarrell were athletic little black boys, but I needed more than just their physical help to pull off what I was attempting. I needed them to use their voices, and charisma. I could not be the sole driving force behind our controlled chaos. At the top of my voice, I shouted, "Everyone in the front of the circle, I need you to lock arms with one another and lean back against the rest of the crowd!" I was trying to create a more uniform ring for these boys to fight in. No one besides the three referees and two fighters were allowed into my ring.

The two boys, who just a second ago were shoving each other, looked at me in bewilderment. They had never seen such swift organization and management of chaos. Their fumbling, surprised looks convinced the crowd that there would not be a fight, and a few people started to disperse. But Jarrell began shouting to get everyone interested again.

"Knock his ass out," Jarrell screamed at one of the boys. "He stole five dollars from you. You gon' take it back or what?"

Jarrell had definitely added fuel to the fire, but he had not yet pushed the boys into fighting. While Tarrell was managing the crowd, I was ready to play chief referee to a fight I was afraid might not happen. Jarrell, the chief instigator, had another trick up his sleeve: He picked up the black boy's arm and threw it at the Hispanic boy's face in order to force a fight. The blow landed with an open hand, and did little damage, but it was all we needed to start the show.

The Hispanic boy threw a rapid combo of punches that landed with a vibrato that sent the crowd into a frenzy. The black boy then sunk one devastating punch into the belly of his opponent, which knocked the wind out of the Hispanic boy. I stood between the fighters to prevent the black boy from landing any cheap shots while the Hispanic boy was recovering. After a few seconds, the Hispanic boy was ready to re-engage. He spat at the floor near the black boy's feet, and I moved out of the way to allow the fight to continue. The black boy had been shadow-boxing while he waited, and now he had his chance. We were ready to see the black boy's flurry of punches that would surely do some permanent damage. But none of those punches ever landed, because the fight was already over. A giant NFL lineman-sized black man had suddenly bulldozed his way through the crowd like a rhinoceros and pushed both boys onto the blacktop. It was Mr. Jamerson, the most senior physical education teacher at the school. He had the strength to shut down a hundred little trouble-makers at once.

Jarrell, Tarrell, and I dispersed with the rest of the crowd. We relinquished all responsibility for our actions as we blended into the stampede of students rushing toward our classrooms. The bell had just rung, and I'd had enough excitement to last me a lifetime. It was time for me to once again bury my head in a mountain of books. I would not know the true consequences of my actions until several days later.

### The Hell I Created

As I clambered out of my classroom for the cafeteria, my ears were assaulted by frighteningly loud screams. I noticed that hazy smoke filled the air. From the second-story balcony, I was shocked to see a whole army of cops outside the academic building. Our school only had one or two police officers regularly on duty. I thought I'd walked into a war zone. I had to descend down the concrete stairs into this chaos—a series of battles between students and police officers.

I could not wrap my head around what was happening. When I tried to enter the cafeteria, I was confronted by a wall of police officers with riot shields who were spraying pepper spray and launching tear gas grenades at the students. I was standing between four sets of students engaging in separate fights, and there was no way the police would allow me to pass them, for fear that I was trying to flank them in order to attack someone else.

Groups of Hispanic kids were fighting groups of black kids. It dawned on me that this was a race war.

I started to think I had fueled this race war by causing that basketball court fight a few days prior. Probably all of this tension had been building up for quite some time, but I was blind to it, until it was too late.

I wondered what side of this race riot I was on. Who would I fight? I was half-Hispanic myself, being Afro-Cuban on my mom's side. But while Spanish was my mother's first language, she never taught it to me. Besides, I looked just like the rest of the black boys who were beating up my Hispanic brothers. Was I supposed to help whichever side was currently losing?

These fights were nothing like any of the brawls I had ever been in. The participants felt a deep fear and hatred toward one another just because of the color of their opponents' skin. They had turned each other into the "other," and were trying to do serious damage. The police were not able to handle all the fights at the same time, so they focused on stopping the fights that involved weapons first. A couple of the school's gang members were escalating the fights by throwing rocks or bashing people over the head with metal scooters. The cops quickly tackled and subdued the gangs. I ran outside to escape the smoke clouds of tear gas.


"Everyone go back to your classrooms! Lunch is over! Stop fighting and go back to your classrooms!" The loudspeaker system was barely audible over the commotion engulfing the school.

As I passed two kids who were fighting, a police officer squirted them with pepper spray. A small amount landed on my collar. I had been coughing violently before this, but this new irritant on my collar made my eyes water. Breathing became even more difficult.

At the base of the stairwell, I saw a fair-skinned, curly-haired kid with a huge, goofy smile. I vaguely knew him. This kid was one year below me in the school, and he was in the same academic program that I was in. His racial background was a lot more ambiguous than mine. But it seemed he knew his role in this race war—to save his friends. He gestured that he wanted to help, so I leaned on him as he carried me up the stairs and out of the chaos for the relative safety of my classroom. I thanked my rescuer, but never got his name.

Random kid / friend whose name I forget.

## My Trespasses Were Forgiven, as I Forgave Those Who Trespassed Against Me

The next few days at Audubon Middle School were tense. The whole school population seemed to have intentionally segregated itself. Since I felt responsible for the racial war, I felt I would have to make amends. I would have to reconnect the two sides. When the bell rang to start our lunch period one day, I told Jarrell and Tarrell to follow me once more. I had a plan.

Most of the Hispanics who played sports would be on the grass fields at lunch playing soccer. The black kids were on the blacktop playing basketball. My plan was this: to reintegrate these groups by using the camaraderie they enjoyed from playing sports together. That shared love would bleed into our social groups off the playground, as well. All I needed to do was form my team of friends to make it all happen.

My buddies Sergio, Christian Cruz, Eric Sanchez, Jarell, and Tarrell all had my back. We started off on the grass fields trying to play soccer with everyone. I had never played the sport before, and was only slightly better than average, so I passed the ball quickly before I caused myself further embarrassment. That was the first time I had ever played a sport with no intention of winning. This time, I was there to unite people.

Soon I was able to lure a fair number of the black kids to play soccer with our Hispanic brothers. Uniting the races was going well, but a bunch of my black friends had no interest in soccer. These boys only wanted to play basketball, so to accomplish my goal I would have to bring some of my new Hispanic friends onto the basketball courts.

They adapted to playing basketball a lot faster than I had adapted to playing soccer. These games were a lot more competitive, as my black friends never held back on me for being on "the wrong team." My mixed bag of teammates could win a few games, but we almost always got pushed off the court by the best teams.

Every day we would come back to the basketball courts, eager to try our luck once more to beat some of the best players on the playground. It was going to be a long process, but I was going to get everyone on the blacktop to respect my teammates and see them for who they really were. In order to even come close to my goal, I would have to play my heart out. If I was not carrying the team, we would not stand a chance at winning most games. I also understood the importance of utilizing my team, though. Many of them did not speak English, so communicating the true complexities of basketball was essentially impossible. If two or three people were guarding me, I needed my other four teammates to be ready to take a shot when I passed them the ball.

"Mauricio, just shoot the damn ball. Shoot it! Shoot it!"

The time was running out in the lunch period, and we were so close to our biggest victory. All I had to do was run down the court and score the game-winning point. I sprinted as fast as I could, gliding down the court with only one of my opponents even remotely fast enough to keep up. When I elevated myself into the air to take the shot, I was already flying toward the basket at full speed. I thought that I might have the opportunity to turn this layup into a dunk (my first dunk). But it never happened. My opponent and

I collided midair, and a flash of red confetti filled the air to celebrate my defeat. My shot had been blocked, and as there was no such thing as a foul on the blacktop, the game was over. We landed on our backs just as the school bell rang.

When I got up to congratulate my opponent, I saw he was covered in blood. I asked him if he was OK as I started to yell at the crowd that he needed medical help. The boy just stared at me as he frantically pointed at my head.

The blood was not my opponent's; it was mine. I had cracked my head open, and blood was gushing everywhere. I looked at the blood-soaked palm of my hand. It was like taking a hot shower and having every part of your body hugged by a warm abundance of liquid. Mauricio, my teammate who barely spoke English, tore off a piece of his shirt and started wrapping it around my head. I trusted this Mexican boy; I knew he was trying to save my life.

Everyone around me seemed to be losing their minds as they scrambled to get more towels, more adults, more help. The whole scene reminded me of the first part of my favorite poem, "If" by Rudyard Kipling. It starts, "If you can keep your head when all about you are losing theirs and blaming it on you ..." Everyone was going crazy, but I was keeping a cool head. No one was more relaxed about this *emergency* than me. I was reciting my favorite poem over and over in my head. My eighth grade teacher, Ms. May, would never believe me if I told her I cracked my head open and lost the poem she'd forced us to memorize or fail her class.

Finally, a stampede of adults came to scoop me up and take me to the nurse's office. For some reason, the school thought my mother would be available to come pick me up.

Eventually my father came to the school to transport me to the hospital. I had bled through several towels and shirts by that point, but for the most part I was stable. Until that day, I never knew how much blood the human body could lose without passing out. But now I knew it was enough to take a decent shower in. My father had not lived with me for some time. He and my mother separated after Kumasi was born. But he answered the call when the school needed an emergency contact. My father was very old and sickly, but he would not allow declining health to stand in the way of protecting his favorite son.

There was another reason for his paying extra attention to me: I was always getting into fights. He and I had a ritual where he would pick me up from school after a fight. As long as I had won the fight, there would be no punishment. I think he liked my fighting spirit because he was something of a fighter himself. He was a very good boxer back in his day, almost going professional. My father enjoyed hearing about my fights. I'm sorry he didn't live long enough to be ringside at my boxing matches in college. Who wouldn't want to see their son become a heavy-weight All-American boxer?

This time was different, though. My father thought I'd been in a fight even though the school officials said that I had an accident on the basketball courts. My father did not believe their story. He always favored himself as someone who could read between the lines. On the way to the hospital that day, he needed to ask me a question that mattered more than anything else to him.

"Ajamu, did you win the fight?"

I stared, bewildered at this man as he drove us down the highway. I was holding a mess of bloody rags around my head. He thought that if there was a fight, then there was some possibility that I had won—even in my condition. I knew this would probably be one of the last times I would ever see him because he was dying. But I hated the idea of lying to him. I kept quiet, trying to think of a way out of this.

He asked me the question once again. I suddenly had an angle: I had been involved in a fight for racial justice. And I had won.

I decided to open my mouth and tell him the only truth he was prepared to hear.

"Sir, I lost the basketball game but won the real fight."

He leaned over to bounce his fist off my chest a few times.

"Damn straight you won the fight, Ajamu!"

He smiled all the way to the hospital.

# Chapter 5
## Losing Everything in the Jungles

**Basketball**

HE LIVED IN the Jungles too!

I met a new friend at the end of my last year at Audubon Middle school. He told me he lived in the Jungles, a little far away from Audubon. The two of us had already become formidable on the basketball court in 2v2 matches, and he wanted me to come play ball with him outside of school. Rodney Savannah explained that he wanted to take me to Jim Gilliam Park, and I told him that was my usual place for games. He was excited that we lived in the same neighborhood.

"Yeah, dude. I go there all the time," I said. "But I've never seen you there."

"Yohancé," Rodney said plainly, "that's because I don't play with the people our age."

Rodney was inviting me to play with the crowd I usually avoided in the Jungles. I was game. Jim Gilliam Park became the place where Rodney and I started hustling people out of their pocket money by playing a little basketball. I would never have done this when I was younger. I was too intimidated. But things were changing, and I was changing. Puberty had dropped on me like a ton of bricks; I started to look five years older than I was. My body frequently ached from growing so fast, and it seemed I woke up with new muscles. No longer did I have to play on the kids' side of the basketball courts; I was big enough to run with the adults. My height and large frame gave people the impression that I was a force to be reckoned with on the court. I stampeded down the lane and aggressively fought for every basket. My opponents liked my rough style of play. They would say, "This is streetball on the blacktop, and there ain't no room for sissies here!" We weren't a bunch of millionaires parading around a fancy waxed gymnasium; we were a bunch of roughnecks who never called our fouls.

The problem was that Rodney, despite being fairly tall, was kinda flimsy lookin'. It was a bright and sunny Saturday morning, and everyone was ready to go. They were on the sidelines, sizing up the competition. Our competition consisted of grown men who were either gangbangers or small-time hustlers.

Little did they know that Rodney was the real secret weapon. Yeah, he was skinny, but Rodney was agile, creative, and extremely lucky. Rodney would throw the ball in ways that seemed stupid, nonchalant, and goofy; and yet it would always go into the basket. By the end of the match-up, people would stop guarding me and only focus on Rodney. Every move he made appeared effortless. Rodney embarrassed every man aspiring to be the best baller in the Jungles, prompting roars of laughter from the spectators. One of the gangbangers we played was getting furious at Rodney for making him look so bad. He pulled out a stack of money and started making small bets that Rodney couldn't repeat any of the amazing shots that he has already pulled off. Rodney, of course, made every shot: behind-the-back shots, one-handed shots, repeated half-court shots. The gangbanger watched his stack disappear quickly—into Rodney's pocket.

Suddenly the gangbanger announced that the game was over and that he now wanted to play Rodney in a one-on-one game for five hundred dollars. This was approximately the amount he had just lost. As I moved to the sidelines of the court, I could feel something bad was about to happen. A large crowd of men, dressed head to toe in red, were now laughing at Rodney and telling their friend to make it quick. These gangbangers were Bloods. Even though I knew a few of them, the guy playing Rodney was a new face. He must have recently gotten out of jail, because everyone called him by this name I had been hearing for months, Big Blood. Everybody and they momma had been talking about Big Blood getting out of jail soon.

Rodney got the ball first and performed a dribbling move called the slip-and-slide. Big Blood literally almost broke his ankle trying to guard Rodney as the first point was scored. Hobbling back to the top of the key, Big Blood passed the ball back. Rodney dribbled the ball low and playfully in front of his opponent, grinning widely. Suddenly, Big Blood smacked Rodney in the face, snatched the ball, and ran to the basket to get his first point. The Bloods on the sideline began cheering for their leader. Instinctively, I took a step onto the court but was met by loud commands to get back.

"You gotta be tougher den that! Caint be bitch made and let a lil smack stop yo game!" said Big Blood.

It appeared he wanted to teach Rodney a lesson by smacking him up and down the court. Rodney was struck with every shot he took. I watched the whole game as my friend devolved from joyfully playing the sport he loved to fighting back tears with a swollen face covered in welts. And I could do nothing but stand on the sideline, paralyzed.

Looking across the court, I tried to find a few familiar faces among the Bloods—guys that might help me put an end to this shit. The ones I knew were some good dudes, the one's I'd met at the ice-cream truck. That bright Saturday morning on the basketball courts with Rodney in trouble is where I decided I needed to cash in my favor with these Bloods. I walked around to the north side of the court, a kid with a white tattered T-shirt, wading through the sea of red.

"What's up, mini Mike Tyson?" said a guy I recognized.

"Mini Mike Tyson! What's good, ma nigga!?" another chimed in.

I had found the Bloods from the ice cream truck. I explained quickly that my friend was getting assaulted by Big Blood, and I needed it to stop. They cut me cold and said that wasn't going to happen. Just then, Rodney looked frantically at me, saw I was talking to the Bloods, and couldn't figure out why I was on their side of the court. He must have thought I was siding with the red team and having fun at his expense. He stared at me with hurt and outrage; Rodney believed I had betrayed him while I really was attempting to help.

The minute they refused to intervene, I realized that those gangbangers were not my friends. But Rodney was. Rodney was the one who would be taking every honors and Advanced Placement course at Crenshaw High with me in the fall. He'd be the one pushing me in all the classes we share because we have the same goal: graduate and get out of the hood. None of the Bloods shared our vision. Their pinnacle of success consisted of becoming Big Blood, a path I had already decided against. Right now, I had to convince Rodney that we were still on the same team.

At the end of the game, Big Blood told Rodney and me that we might be tough enough to join their gang. He offered us a jump-in: We would fight twenty Bloods all at one time. At the end of the fight, we would be a part of their gang. Rodney looked over at me as if to say it was my call, but I had made this decision a long time ago. I put my arm around Rodney and politely declined to the Bloods for both of us. They didn't seem bothered by my decision. To them I was turning down a really good deal, but I knew better. Right as I told them no, Rodney lurched from under my arm, pushed me to the ground, and started walking home. The gang laughed and jeered at us. I grabbed Rodney's basketball and headed after him.

Rodney only lived a few blocks away from the park, so I walked with him to make sure he got home safe. We did not speak to each other the entire time. I realized that if Rodney had decided to prematurely end that charade of a game that his attacker was calling a lesson, we both would have been in serious danger. But I didn't care because if Rodney had defended himself just once, I would have jumped in and died for him that day. About halfway to his apartment building, Rodney's eyes started to overflow. His tears must have stung his welted face. He wasn't crying just because he was sad; he was in pain. We said goodbye at the front gate to his building and after I turned around, I started to cry too.

## My Home

My little brother Kumasi was the luckiest when it came to finding money. Most weekends we would walk to the public library to hop on a computer. We had to get out of our apartment for several reasons, primarily to find food. We always had a better chance walking the streets of Los Angeles than looking in our barren kitchen cabinets. At this point, our mom was rarely home. We never knew if she had been readmitted to a mental hospital or was roaming the streets again. It was time for us to take care of ourselves, and what better age to start than fourteen? Playing video games on computers at the library was fun; Kumasi and I did it to escape from our problems. But it sucked playing on an empty stomach. Kumasi was always on the lookout for loose change, and he looked everywhere—even under the library computer mousepad.

I looked at him like he was crazy, but Kumasi explained he had found five dollars there yesterday and was guessing he might find more today. While I was trying to make money with Rodney the day before, Kumasi was in a library having a much easier time. The boy was just that darn lucky. Every time he found money, it meant that we could eat that day.

One day, we were walking home from the library, a fairly long walk down Martin Luther King Jr. Boulevard. We were in a deep discussion about Runescape, the videogame we had just spent hours playing at the library.

"You need level 43 prayer to pray for protection from melee, so it wouldn't work, niglet," I told Kumasi.

Out of the corner of my eye, I caught a glimpse of a stranger rapidly approaching. After sizing him up, I concluded that he was looking for a fight, so today was the day that this man was going to get beat down. By me. I didn't want Kumasi to participate in this fight; he was the worst fighter. The man was now in front of us.

"Are you two talking about prayer?" he asked.

"No sir, we are talking about a video game," I said. "Right, Kumasi?"

"Naa ..." he said, unafraid of the strange man. Kumasi reached down and picked up a crumpled piece of paper at his feet. "I'm talking about this twenty-dollar bill I just found on the ground."

The man looked annoyed and just walked away. The whole situation confused me so much that I missed my opportunity to cross the street when the light changed. Had that man actually thought we were talking about prayer and wanted to join our conversation? Or did he want the twenty-dollar bill for himself? And where was all this money for Kumasi coming from? Surely the streets of South Central Los Angeles are not covered in free money.

After we crossed the street, Kumasi and I did talk about prayer briefly. I told him I believe in God and that I pray. He told me he didn't pray, but that he believed in whatever higher power kept blessing him with these dollars.

But Kumasi's money luck wasn't a twenty-four-hour thing. So I would occasionally steal a few small items from the grocery store. I felt awful and stupid every time I stole. There must be a better way to do something so simple as feeding yourself. Eventually we tried the whole "asking for help" thing out. A few adults we knew bought groceries for us. But when they brought them to our apartment, they had so many questions:

*Where is your mother?*

*You know you have an eviction notice outside your door, right?*

*Are you sure you are going to be OK?*

I wanted to bellow back at them, "Yes, we're OK. After all, I'm the man of the house! Leave us alone." But I didn't sass back these generous people. Instead, I nodded, smiled, politely thanked them … and refused to answer their questions. These instances made me realize I don't like taking charity. My mom had never had problems taking charity, so I'd benefited from it my whole life. But to ask for it myself crushed my heart and soul. I remember one dinner after a neighbor brought us food, I cried as I ate a giant salami. I had not earned this meal. It was given to me because I was less than everyone else. I needed help.

A few days later my mother finally showed up. I asked her permission to go to a friend's house for the weekend. She told me that she and Kumasi might not be in this apartment when I got back; she had just been accepted at a shelter a few hours away. I told her that I was too smart, good-looking, and charismatic to be homeless. My mom laughed at me and told me I had already been homeless for quite some time.

Though I had heard it so frequently from others growing up, hearing that insult from my mother hurt much worse. Kids used to tease me all the time about my raggedy clothes and the holes in them. They would call me a bum, dirty, or homeless, but I learned to laugh at myself. These kids didn't know what they were saying was actually true. But when my mom said it to me, it struck me square in my heart. Wasn't she the person who was supposed to take care of me and make sure I wasn't a bum, I wasn't dirty, and I wasn't homeless? In small doses my mother could be my favorite person in the world. But she had definitely overstayed her welcome this time—and she had just arrived. I didn't have concrete plans as to which friend's house I was going to stay at, but I knew I had to leave before I said or did something I might regret. I packed up my bags and left the apartment that day feeling I'd lost everything in the Jungles.

# Chapter 6
## Sneaking onto the Best Football Team

THE SUMMER OF 2007 had come and gone. It was early September now and because I was so focused on not being homeless, I had never gone to summer football practice at my new high school. I was getting pretty good at couch-surfing between friends' houses, but I needed a sure place to sleep every night before joining the team. My best friend Kolmus let me stay for a while since we were both headed to Crenshaw High. But by the time I had what I needed, the school year had already started, and the chances of being let onto the team now were slim to none.

It was a hot day on the playground at Crenshaw High. I was a few weeks into my freshman year, and I hated Physical Education class; I didn't belong in there. Football players were not required to take P.E. classes, and I was supposed to be one of them. My best friend Kolmus and I came in first or second place in any physical challenge this class put in front of us. Kolmus was a big Nigerian boy I'd known since we first met in kindergarten. Puberty was blessing him in much the same way it had done for me. Together we looked like the Monstarz from *Space Jam* playing against the *Looney Tunes* cast that was the rest of our class. Today was going to be different though, because we were going to have a substitute teacher. Kolmus and I were in pretty much every class together, and he found out that the substitute was one of the football coaches. Kolmus and I were going to try and convince the coach to switch us out of this P.E. class and onto the football team.

Coach Ace, a fit and professional-looking man, began the class with roll call. When he reached my name, he paused, then pointed at me and asked, "Are you a Salimu?" Even though he had never seen me before, he must have spotted me because I looked like my siblings who were either currently at the school or had been in the past. I jumped the gun and explained that I wanted to be out of this class and on the football team. Coach Ace said he would take care of me after roll call.

Kolmus and I followed Coach Ace to the football office to request a change in our schedules. I tried to give as few details to the coach as possible, because if he knew the whole story, he would not be doing us such a big favor. Coach Ace must have thought that two of their football players were accidentally placed in a P.E. class. Kolmus and I looked the part, so we didn't have to answer many questions, just smile and nod.

After school was over, it was time for Kolmus and me to plan our heist.

"We must be the two biggest guys at this school who are not on the football team, Yohancé. Why are we not on the team yet?" Kolmus asked me. I had been staying at Kolmus's house for a few days now, and I had my reasons why I had not shown up for summer practice. It was time to stop making excuses and join already.

"Do you think he will let us join the team late? We missed all of their summer practice," Kolmus said to me.

"Who are you talking about?" I asked.

"G-Man, Yohancé! G-Man! The head coach everyone is so afraid of," spouted Kolmus.

"I think I can sneak onto the team, and if you follow me, we could just blend in like we belong."

"That is either the smartest or the dumbest idea I have ever heard, Yohancé," Kolmus said.

"Yeah, man, we already got our schedules changed. All we gotta do now is keep showing up and act like we've always been there," I told Kolmus.

"But what if he spots us and starts beating us in front of everyone? I know it sounds crazy, but I heard he hits all of his players when they do something stupid. That's why the team is so good and disciplined. I'm not trying to catch the smackdown today," Kolmus said.

"He won't hit you, Kolmus. He only goes that far with the kids whose families he knows very well and has been given permission to be a father figure to. He will probably hit me, though, because one of my older brothers is a senior on the varsity team. G-Man calls my family 'the Salimu clan.' I have never met the man, but I have heard stories from my older brothers. The second I say my full name, he will know that he's got another son."

When school was over, Kolmus and I hopped the back fence to enter the football field from a more discreet location. Hundreds of boys were spread out across the field in a uniform stretching formation. There were ten columns of boys that stretched all the way from goal line to goal line. At the front of the formation stood G-Man with a bullhorn. G-Man was a big black man with powerful arms and a belly so big that it served as another weapon in his arsenal to punish you with. He wore aviator sunglasses—always—and his hair wildly shot out in every direction from under his baseball cap. Even though he was carrying a bullhorn, none of the earth-shaking commands were coming from G-Man. Every new command to perform a stretch came from the giant standing next to him. This NFL-bound, muscle head, skyscraper of a man yelled so loudly that Kolmus and I jumped and scurried into formation to do as we were told.

"Who are you guys?" a boy stretching next to us whispered.

"Just guys joining the football team," I whispered back. I couldn't give anyone my name just yet.

RIGHT FOOT FORWARD!!!

STRETCH!!!

If he yelled any louder, my eardrums would have popped. We were doing the stretches, why did he need to scare his team during a warm-up?

LEFT FOOT FORWARD!!!

STRETCH!!!

"You know who that is, right?" Kolmus whispered to me as he pointed in the direction of the giant.

"Yes, I do, and I always hate when he yells at me," I whispered back.

RIGHT KNEE DOWN! LEFT LEG UP!!!

STRETCH!!!

The giant was part of the Salimu clan. He was Abasi, my older brother and captain of this football team.

"Little Abasi is that you? You got big," one of the varsity players loudly whispered to me across the field.

I had met that guy years ago when my older brother still lived in the same home as me. He must have recognized me. I didn't miss living with Abasi. He was a ravenous eater and would have caused my death by starvation if he hadn't moved out.

"Little Abasi?" whispered a random voice in the crowd.

"Little Abasi???" echoed a few more players further away, and closer to G-Man and my brother.

LEFT KNEE DOWN! RIGHT LEG UP!!!

STRETCH!!!

The whispering chorus of "little Abasi" echoed through the warm-up stretches. I was sure that Kolmus and I would be discovered soon enough. Surely G-Man and Abasi heard the commotion, but no one was pulled out of formation. Usually, talking during this stretching formation would result in G-Man paying someone a visit—and being generous to them. That meant he would offer them the people's elbow, or maybe some sweet chin music. If he saw me, he might save all of that generosity for me as punishment for crashing his practice.

Whistles began blowing, and a whole commotion of movement happened; the wall of players parted and then Coach JG emerged and started yelling at me. He said that JV was to go to snacks and film, while varsity would stay on the field for drills. I assumed I was a JV guy and Coach JG was telling me to hurry off the field. I sprinted away with the pack of boys heading toward the locker room.

I must have been running too fast, even though I wasn't trying to attract attention, and the next thing I heard was, "Speedy Gonzales! Pump your brakes!" It was G-Man, and he was heading in my direction. Kolmus stayed behind with me.

"Who … are you?" G-Man bellowed at me.

"My name is Yohancé. It rhymes with Beyoncé, starts with a Y. YOH-HON-SAY," I told G-Man.

"YOH-HON-SAY, what is your full name?" G-Man asked.

Whenever I say my full name, in my head there is always a chorus of African drums playing in the background. This is entirely in my head, but I feel like it is a big deal to say my full name.

"My full name is YOHANCÉ, AJAMU, EBU, SALIMU." (Dadoom Da Doom Doom)

"Another SAUH-LEE-MOO!? How many of you guys are there?" G-Man shot back.

"Currently, there are sixteen siblings and we all share one—if not two—parents," I told G-Man.

"Your brother, Abasi, told me there are only fourteen children, YOH-HON-SAY," G-Man sneered back at me, staring me down.

"Abasi is big and stupid, and he can't count," I informed the coach. "My mother had another baby this summer, and now there are sixteen of us, sir."

"YO-HON-SAY, do not call me sir. Call me G-Man. What do you mean, she had another baby?"

"G-Man, she got pregnant and had another son that we had to give up for adoption," I explained.

"I understand, YOH-HON-SAY. Stand still for me, please," G-Man requested. "Stick your chest out and flex."

He made a fist and systematically tapped on my chest, abdomen, back, and calves as he circled me.

"Who would win in a fight, you or your brother, Abasi?" he asked.

"I have beaten him up before, G-Man. I just tend to lose more often than I win against that monster," I shrugged.

"That's good enough for me," G-Man said with a smile. He looked me in the eye. "You can join this Crenshaw High School football team."

Kolmus raised his goofball hand to show G-Man he had been standing there the whole time. He said quickly, to make his case, "My name is Kolmus. Yohancé is currently staying with me. I was wondering if that football team invitation included a plus one."

G-Man looked a bit confused, but then smiled and nodded, adding, "Snacks are in the back of the locker room. The door to the film room is the last one on your left. And tell Coach Price and Coach Neely that G-Man said you two are now on the JV team."

We had done it. Kolmus and I had successfully snuck onto the best football team in Los Angeles.

# Chapter 7
# Kicking It with Kolmus

KOLMUS WAS ECSTATIC about me staying with him for an extended period of time. Even though we'd known each other since kindergarten, we'd never spent much time together outside of school. This, I found out, was because Kolmus's real address was a secret. The house I thought he lived in was actually a front so that he could go to school in my school district. Homeless kids like me were never locked to a school district because at the drop of a hat we could be living halfway across town—in another shelter. But now Kolmus was ready to show me his real house.

Kolmus's parents were from Nigeria, hardworking and career-driven folks who ran a very orderly household. All three sons were very large, which made me wonder if I would have to fight for food like I did at home. Kolmus and his brothers were well-fed and well-clothed. This was a life I could get used to. I was really grateful; I told Kolmus that his parents had saved me from being homeless. This was a topic I had never discussed with him before.

My buddy had always been the class clown and the first to rip on me for my dirty and tattered clothes. The irony that all of his jokes were true only made him rip on me more now. I liked that about him; he never pitied me.

Unlike the home I grew up in, Kolmus's parents' house had fancy vases, paintings, furniture, cutlery, and fine china. The boys tended to fight like boys do, which meant they risked knocking over beautiful and fragile pieces. I pledged that I would try to calm them down so that there were no broken items. If we did any damage to the house, everyone would be in trouble, and I might find myself out on the street.

The television in the living room was amazingly large. At home, ours was six inches wide, meaning I had to fight Abasi and Kumasi to get a good view of programs. But at Kolmus's house, things were different. I could recline on the lavish black leather sofa across the living room and stare into this crystal-clear portal of entertainment.

One day while watching TV, I suddenly heard a glass vase shatter. The youngest brother, Chimi, twelve at the time, had been fighting the eldest brother, Nkem, who was seventeen. As I took my eyes off the television, I saw a horrific scene that caused me to leap off the couch. Snot was dripping down Chimi's nose, and tears were streaming from his eyes. But more shockingly, he clutched a butcher knife, poised to swing it. Kolmus tried to tell jokes to deescalate the whole situation. But no amount of lighthearted banter could stop the conflict.

I decided it was time to intervene. I ran into the nearest bedroom to grab the blankets off a mattress and returned dragging them indiscriminately behind me. Placing my hand on Kolmus's shoulder, I eased him out of the way and entered into the strike zone. For a brief moment I fooled Chimi into thinking I was replacing Kolmus as some sort of mediator. The knife was held out at arm's length and without hesitation I threw the blanket over the blade and began rapidly wrapping it. Then I grabbed hold of the once-dangerous weapon and punched Chimi in the chest. I used the momentum shift of the boy falling back to yank the knife from his hand. With the knife securely wrapped in the blanket, I turned around slowly and walked away. There was no need to fear the youngest brother retaliating by attacking me from behind. There was already a Nigerian powerhouse rushing past me to engage the boy. Both of his brothers grabbed Chimi and shoved him firmly down on the couch for a family therapy session. Every question in that session was followed by a punch.

"You know we love yo stupid ass, right!?" [Punch.]

I sat down on the adjacent couch and watched the entire session work itself out. I decided to hold on to the knife for a while longer. When the tension finally subsided, the four of us cleaned the house and pretended the broken vase never existed.

I'm not sure about Chimi, but I learned a lot from that family therapy session. Most of what Kolmus's eldest brother Nkem said eventually became principles that I applied to my relationship with Abasi. I didn't want to kill Abasi, and at the end of the day we were on the same team. I still wanted to fight my brothers at times, but I would never think to pull a weapon on them.

It took a little time to adjust to the rules of my new family. I learned that not everything was communal property; sharing always came easy to me, but they did it differently in this household. Certain items were designated to certain individuals, which I found strange. I would get into trouble for eating Chimi's cereal, or Nkem's fish sticks. As I grew more accustomed to living with this family, I would seek to outperform the other boys less and less. When they confronted me about doing their chores, telling me that I had taken their job, I would set the task aside for them to complete. The rule was for me to complete any chore I saw around the house that needed to be done. Kolmus's mom would frequently ask me to do a little more than the other boys.

Eventually I grew so comfortable that I began relaxing my approach to the household rules. I would leave a dish in the sink, or have a drink without a coaster. I did so at the suggestion of the three brothers. I had been living with them for several months, and they said this was now my home. But that was a grave mistake.

In the spring of 2008, Kolmus's mom noticed my new casual attitude and was unhappy; she told me that she thought it best that I return to my own home. She urged me to pack my bags and offered to drive me home. The eldest brother, Nkem, pleaded with his mom, saying it was his fault that I had neglected to wash everyone's dishes the previous night. He had scolded me, saying it was time to stop acting like Cinderella. Ultimately it was my fault, though, because I did not mind doing a hundred times more chores than the rest of the boys. I just wanted to eat, and I should have done those dishes.

The address for my mother's shelter was about three hours away. Kolmus's mom thought it must be incorrect when she programmed her GPS. But off we went. When we arrived, she surveyed the rundown area with shock and her jaw dropped as she began to cry. She kept crying as I grabbed my things from the car. I hugged her and told her it was OK; I'd be OK. I wonder if she would have kicked me out if she knew where I would be headed. I pray that she never reads this book, because IF she did, the next few chapters would break her heart.

# Chapter 8
## No, I Will Not Stay in This Shelter

AS I WALKED through the doors of a massive grey building, I was greeted by my mother. I had two black trash bags slung over my shoulder. The place looked like a huge warehouse with hundreds of cots in a checker patterned across the open floor. My mom told me they had bins under the cots, and that anything I could not store in a bin, I could take to a small security area in the back. The bright lights and cots in open space were already enough for me to want to walk out. But there were also a few strict rules. She recited them:

> You have to leave every morning before 8.
> You can't return to the shelter before 5 p.m.; it's only a place to sleep.
> When they do serve dinner, which isn't always, show up on time or go
>     hungry.
> No matter how hungry you are, only one plate per person.

I told her none of those rules sat right with me; I might have to find other arrangements. She told me all of her children are welcome to do as they please. Kumasi was gone for the next few days as well.

It was the weekend, and I had no idea where to go or what to do to stay busy. I called my girlfriend to come pick me up and stayed at her house for the weekend. I knew that the longer I stayed away from that shelter, the easier it would be to not come back. One of my older sisters, Monifa, had never come back and she was only one year older than me. She was one of the first of my mom's five children to leave home. Monifa had lived on her own since she was twelve years old. The years when our core gang of five lived on Skid Row had turned Monifa into a thug. I could only dream of being as independent as her. Every time I saw Monifa around school, or somewhere in the city, it was a reminder that I too could just leave and never come back. We were grown little kids, and every decision we made was our own.

If I didn't need to look after Kumasi, I probably would have never come back to that shelter. But I needed to know that my little brother was going to be OK, since he was taking care of our mom on his own.

When I saw Kumasi Sunday night, I knew he was thriving just by the smirk on his face. He had grown four inches taller since a few months ago. I couldn't let him stand too close to me for very long, because he was definitely taller than me now. I couldn't bear to have him height check me every ten seconds. Kumasi told me not to worry; he had a system down for taking care of himself and our mom.

I told him I was not ready to call this place my home. He told me he never used that word. Together we agreed to call it "the place," which is what we called every shelter we slept at from then on. It was established as taboo to call a cold and loveless place like this *home*. I was confident that I could leave Kumasi with my mom for a while, but before I left him, I reached into my pocket and gave him half of my money. My girlfriend had given it to me so I could eat meals when I wasn't with her. If Kumasi wasn't eating then neither was I, so I figured half of that money must belong to him.

"Hey, Ajamu. Before you go ... who is this new girlfriend I don't know about?" Kumasi asked.

"Niglet, you never know anything about any of my girlfriends," I said. The big grin on Kumasi's face said it all. He thought I was about to spill the beans.

"Maybe I'll tell you more about this one later," I said to Kumasi. "Peace."

# Chapter 9
## Just Another Crenshaw Cougar

NORMAL. THAT WAS all I wanted to be in high school. I had no issues with self-esteem or peer pressure to do as the cool kids do. When I say normal, I mean being able to blend in with my peers. But behind this big smile and go-getter attitude, I was hiding a reality: I was homeless. The big black duffle bag slung over my shoulder was not to hold my sports equipment. I carried my whole life in that thing. Shirts, pants, underwear, books, deodorant, toothbrushes, and wet wipes. There was never a guarantee of where I would end up on any given night, so I had to be prepared to sleep anywhere. I thought I was doing a really good job at hiding my real circumstances. To students and teachers, I wanted to seem like just another Crenshaw Cougar.

Sometimes I was able to fool people into thinking I was even better than normal. A small crowd of girls walked beside me one day in the hallway, gossiping and laughing as if they wanted me to overhear them. Our lunch period had just started, and I wanted to hurry to the lunchroom. After I ate my meal, I would usually stuff my duffle bag with food that would more than likely be my dinner. Usually I would stop to chat with these girls, but that day I was on a mission. Then one of them called my name.

"Yohancé!? That's you, right?" I turned around to face the girl who had called my name.

"Hi, Yohancé, I'm Tristan. The captain of ..."

"The captain of the cheerleading team," I interrupted.

Why would I not know the prettiest and most popular girl in my high school? I may have been an underclassman, but I wasn't a fool. The girls behind Tristan started to giggle even louder at my quick retort. I smiled and asked if there was anything they needed from me. I didn't intend to be mean; I was just hungry.

"Yohancé, I just wanted to meet you," Tristan continued, her smile growing wider. "I know that you are dating Jennifer, the captain of the dance team. She is a really close friend of mine. So I just wanted to say hi."

"Tristan, we broke up a while ago."

Upon hearing that, Tristan smiled devilishly and asked if that meant I was single. Wow!

It was already a miracle that I had dated one of the most popular upperclassmen in my high school. I couldn't imagine having that miracle repeat itself.

Most of my peers still refuted my story that I met my ex-girlfriend at a party. They said the whole sequence of events just seemed too unlikely. I was at a high school party, just a freshman among upperclassmen. But I walked to the center of the dance floor and grabbed the prettiest girl I could find and just started dancing with her.

By the end of the night I had her phone number and I had a new girlfriend.

The next week in school, everyone saw the lucky son-of-a-gun freshman with the upperclassman girl, the captain of the dance team hotty-hot-hotty on his arm. But that felt like a long time ago. It didn't even last long. Jennifer was pretty cool, but it just wasn't that serious.

If Tristan did become my next girlfriend, I would be a legend at Crenshaw High School. Unfortunately, I was not single at the time, and I told Tristan that I'd already had another girlfriend for some time now. I then rushed to the cafeteria to get my free lunch.

There were multiple places in the school to find a free meal, so after raiding the cafeteria, I usually went to the football offices where G-Man might have some extra food that had been picked over by his team of growing boys. The football season was over, and the Crenshaw weight room was open and ready to turn next year's team into muscled beasts. Only seniors who were going on to play football in college came to work out after the season, but that meant most of them. If there was not enough food to feed everyone lifting weights in the gym, then seniors would go hungry because they were the lowest priority.

On one of the days when there was not enough food, I snuck back into the locker room to scarf down one of the last meals on G-Man's desk. I didn't want anyone to know I had eaten when they hadn't. I especially didn't want them to see me eating the team's food, because there was a rumor floating around that I would not be playing football next year. I didn't want to explain to everyone why I couldn't play football my sophomore year. I was too embarrassed to admit that I was homeless and needed help. Instead, I would just drop responsibilities off my plate—namely football.

When I entered the locker room, I took a seat on a narrow bench. I was halfway through a massive turkey sandwich when my brother Abasi entered. I sat my sandwich down neatly and prepared to defend my lunch.

"Scoot over," Abasi commanded in a voice too nice to be his own. He reached into his locker and grabbed his phone.

"What do you think about her?" he asked, showing me a girl my age on his phone.

"She's ugly, bro, and a little young for you," I teased Abasi.

"This is my girl's little sister," he shot back. "I need you to come on a double-date with me. I'm just showing you her picture as a courtesy."

I told him I needed more details to understand. My brother then explained to me that this was online dating. He had never met this girl in person. They had planned to see a movie. She felt that if she brought her little sister and Abasi brought his little brother, then everything would work out. I told Abasi I had a girlfriend already—but that I would think about it.

Being a procrastinator would frequently cause me to fail. I seldom had access to a computer to complete my assignments for class. My peers were advancing in school thanks to leveraging new high-tech tools that would accomplish more in less time. Eventually my school realized what a great disadvantage I was in and issued me a school laptop. Until then, I completed most of my assignments on a cellphone.

My cellphone in that day was pretty basic; I never had access to programs like simulations for my Biology class or videos for Trigonometry. Not even word processing software. I used long text messages to write essays. There were computers at my school, but I only used those to spellcheck and format my work—and I was rushing to finish assignments hours before they were due. I had no excuse to not complete my assignments. If I needed six hours to complete an assignment but could only find two hours to spend in the library, I made up for the missing four hours by borrowing someone else's smart phone. Eventually I graduated to using my own smart phone. When I finally saved enough money to get my own, I vowed I would never miss turning in an assignment on time again.

I can still remember those words from my English teacher Ms. Hanson: "Yohancé, until you become some fancy famous author, you will have to follow all of the literary rules. Including turning your work in on time."

The culture of kids always being on their cellphones in class was just starting when I was in high school. If I was sitting in a classroom that I did not feel like I was learning in, then I would pull out my cellphone and work on coursework from other classes. But I was seen as just another kid slacking off in class. My Spanish teacher was very resistant to this type of behavior, and one day I felt the need to challenge her. I had a six-page paper on the Holocaust due within two hours, and I just had to write a final conclusion. I told my teacher my intentions at the beginning of her class, but she must have forgotten. She caught me and two classmates on our phones and took them all. So I never got to finish my paper and earned a rotten grade.

That experience in my Spanish class nearly broke my will to work my way up. I knew that a black man must work twice as hard to succeed, but this was ridiculous. Why was I trying so hard, when the walls surrounding me were collapsing? I didn't feel like I was succeeding at even the basics. I couldn't even feed and take care of myself, so how could I expect to complete a stupid paper?

For some dumb reason, I thought that I was the smartest of all my brothers and sisters. But I was failing the hardest. Maybe I had set my sights too high and was doing way too much for a boy in my circumstances. I felt defeated.

# Chapter 10
## The Date I Set My Vector

"ARE YOU EVER going to stop looking so sad," Abasi scolded me, "and make up your mind about going with me on this double-date?"

I had been stalling him for weeks. Instead of giving him a straight answer, I just told him to ask me again later. I finally decided to establish some ground rules with him. I said I would go only if I could take my girl-friend, and not that girl's sister. Surprisingly, he agreed. He said he'd pick me up on Saturday. He just needed to know where I was living.

His last question was really hard to answer. I had been couch-surfing at so many different friends' houses, that I did not know where I would be that weekend. Abasi was staying in a shed in the back of a family friend's house and could be found easily. I, on the other hand, could be anywhere, pretending that I was just having another sleepover with a friend. I told Abasi that I would find him that day and we'd pick up our dates.

Abasi had a car now, and more money than I had ever seen before in my life. Seeing him doing so well further nagged my thoughts; I was the only Salimu struggling.

"How do you know this girl again?" Abasi quizzed me. "And why doesn't she go to Crenshaw High?"

Abasi, like everyone else, was curious about this girl I had been dating for a while. She had been giving me money, buying me clothes, and, according to the stories I had been telling, she was beautiful. She just didn't live in the hood, which is why no one ever saw her. I would talk about her, but never in any great detail. I explained that her name was Janie and that Abasi would meet her that evening.

"Details, man, details!" Abasi seemed to be getting impatient as we drove more than halfway across the city. I loved giving out the details in installments and driving him crazy. It gave me power. I told Abasi that Janie had fair brown skin, long, straight, dark hair, and a thin, athletic build from her days as a cheerleader and a gymnast.

When Abasi pushed for more details, I pushed right back.

"So that's all you're going to tell me about her? Ajamu, you don't see the huge gap of information missing here?"

"I told you this much as a courtesy," I said, throwing his words back at him as we got close to her house. "I just don't want you acting stupid or drooling when you see this beautiful woman."

We arrived in a neighborhood that was far superior to any we had ever lived in. This was the kind of area where you could leave your front door unlocked, or your keys in your car without any fear of carjacking. Abasi stared at me with an accusatory look. For a second I thought he was giving me the people's eyebrow, but his feigned intensity subsided into a chuckle.

I pulled out the new cellphone Janie had just bought me and texted her that we had arrived. Janie didn't walk out of her house, she sort of pranced. She had the cutest smile on her face, and when she was in full view it felt as if all the colors in the world shined brighter. The weather was already perfect in Los Angeles, but when Janie appeared, I swear the sun shined even brighter.

"Be cool," I told Abasi. "You have to close your mouth and stop staring before she gets in the car, bro."

I got out of the car like a gentleman and met Janie in the street with a big hug. Then I formally introduced the two. The two of them smiled and lied about how they had heard so much about each other. Formalities were over and we drove across the city to pick up Abasi's date.

When she got in, it felt a bit awkward between Abasi and her. After all, it was their first in-person date; until now, they had really only ever spoken online or on the phone.

When we arrived at the movie theater, the sun had already begun to set, so I offered Janie the light jacket I was wearing. Abasi somehow saw this as a competition and mimicked my gesture for his date. She declined his offer. I laughed inwardly.

The movie we saw that night was a spy thriller called *Eagle Eye*, starring Shia LeBeouf. Looking back on my life, I realize this film was one of my biggest influences. In the film, two brothers are always competing. But one advances far when he gets a fancy science degree from the United States Air Force Academy (USAFA). He becomes a wing commander. That was the first time I had ever heard of the Academy, and yet, for some reason, I knew that I would be headed there one day. The rest of the night all I could do was focus on my new career goal. I didn't know how I was going to get it done, but nothing had ever felt so sure in my whole life.

# Section 2 / Second Quarter

Back when I was undefeated

*If I wanted something, I had to fight for it!*

# Chapter 11
## Robots for Dinner

I WAS GOING to be a cadet at the Air Force Academy. With a renewed sense of purpose, I focused on my studies even harder now. No longer was motivation an issue; I would do whatever it took to succeed at Crenshaw High School and enter USAFA.

Of course, not everything changed; I still struggled with the issues of where to find my next meal or lay my head at night. I had made new relationships with folks that I could depend on, but I made sure never to be a burden on any one person.

Sure, I could spend extended periods at Janie's house, or other friends' homes, but I never wanted to be given the boot again like I was at Kolmus's house. I would always make sure to leave well before I overstayed my welcome. Many of the people I stayed with tried to convince me that I should stay longer, but I would leave after a certain amount of time—even if I failed to secure a new bed for the night. I simply slept in the stairwells in my high school. That way, I could take advantage of showers, food, and places to study. Staying there overnight never felt like a big deal. Most of my clothes and possessions were either in my big black duffle bag or tucked away in my school locker. Crenshaw High was not just my school—it was my home.

Getting caught lurking in my high school late at night was the most annoying part about being homeless. I would explain that I was just waiting on my parents, or that I needed to stay late to study. If a teacher caught me, this lie usually worked, but the janitorial staff usually made me move out of the way so they could do their cleaning.

One teacher particularly hard to fool was my biology teacher, Dr. Ramsey. The Doc was a bitter and strict old black man, and he always wore a suit and tie. His well-groomed manner had come from his past career as a medical doctor. He would regularly stay at the school until midnight grading papers, and he would leave the air conditioner on in his classroom. During a hot night, this a/c made the outside of Dr. Ramsey's classroom a very desirable spot to be.

One evening, as I lurked in the hallway, Dr. Ramsey suddenly came out to confront me.

"Mr. Salimu, why are you sitting outside of my classroom this late at night?"

"Hello, Dr. Ramsey! I was just, umm ..."

"Sleeping outside my door again," Dr. Ramsey said abruptly. "Mr. Salimu, if you need help with anything, you do understand that all you need do is ask me. Correct?"

"Yes, sir. I must have dozed off because track and field practice was so hard today." I thought I was a wizard when it came to lying, but Dr. Ramsey was not buying my tricks.

"Mr. Salimu, you need to figure out where you are going to sleep to-night, because I will not allow you to snore outside of my door all night. I am going to finish grading these papers, and then I will drop you off somewhere safe. You figure out where you want to go. The choice is yours—Cougar Pride."

It always irked me how often teachers used the school motto to make their point. I get it; we all have choices to make, even Dr. Ramsey. Teachers were not allowed to drive students home. That was against the rules of the Los Angeles Unified School District. But Dr. Ramsey felt a moral obligation. I had him drop me off at a friend's house that night.

From that night on, I had to try harder to evade Dr. Ramsey. But he knew I was still in the building and would look for me before leaving. I think he was tired of catching me, because one evening he lectured me, saying I needed to go stay in the shelter with my mother and little brother, and also that I needed more after-school programs to keep me busy. Dr. Ramsey said that I had the drive to succeed, like many of my siblings. He also told me that I had the smarts and strength to look after my little brother Kumasi. He certainly needed my help. Dr. Ramsey insisted that I needed to be a father figure to my little brother. I needed to pick back up where I had long ago abandoned my post.

As I listened to my teacher's advice, I realized he had led me into another part of the building. Dr. Ramsey pointed at a closed door I had never entered before.

"Mr. Salimu, this is your new after-school activity."

He knocked on a door, which unexpectedly opened despite the late evening.

"Mr. Yohancé, I been expectin' ya fur sum time now," said this tall old man in the heaviest Caribbean accent I had ever heard before. Apparently, Dr. Ramsey had been sharing the details of my homeless situation with other staff members at Crenshaw High, looking for solutions. This new person, Mr. Reis, was going to help. Dr. Ramsey left us alone. Mr. Reis looked at me with excitement and passion in his eyes, as if he had a big secret he couldn't wait to reveal to me.

"Mr. Reis, what kind of after-school activity or club is this?"

"Dis is a robotics club, Yohancé. We build and compete in de biggest robotics competition in de world," he told me.

I looked around. The room was almost empty, except for a few trophies and medals. I picked up one of the medals. It read: *F.I.R.S.T.* and there was a design of a robot engraved in the center. I picked up a couple more. They read the same.

"All of these medals say first," I said. "Do you guys always come in first place worldwide?"

Mr. Reis laughed deeply. "No, no, no, no, boy. We have never dun dat well, Mr. Yohancé. De organization dat runs de whole competition is called F.I.R.S.T., which means: For Inspiration and Recognition of Science and Technology."

Every time Mr. Reis spoke, I would hear a part of the movie *The Little Mermaid* in my head—the song "Under the Sea," because he sounded like the sea crab Sebastian, who also had a heavy Caribbean accent.

Mr. Reis walked me through the second set of double doors to meet the team, and I instantly realized I was in the right place. There were test stations that had been constructed in all four corners of the room, jumbles of batteries and wires. There were piles of wood and scrap metal behind unopened cases of power tools. This team had every resource they needed and only lacked leadership, my leadership.

This robotics team was team #1692, and while they were certainly exposing a lot of kids to technology, they were not doing any winning. The last robot that the team constructed to compete was in the back of the room collecting dust. They had retired it several years ago. Most years the team never finished a robot in time to send one to the regional competitions. I suddenly felt like I could make a difference. I decided that I would be the catalyst to change that.


A group of five boys and girls on the current robotics team was sitting in the center of the room, eating pizza and discussing plans for the upcoming competition. I got a slice of pizza and joined their discussion. After listening to everyone speak, I realized that there really was no leader amongst the group. Without a leader, the team would repeat last year's performance, failing to build a robot in time for competition. I began to introduce myself.

"Hello everyone, my name is Yohancé. Rhymes with Beyoncé, starts with a 'Y.' Yoh-hon-say. And I am going to be your new captain and the leader of this robotics team."

The table erupted in a mixture of sarcastic cheers and loud bouts of laughter, but I was dead serious. I always felt uniquely qualified to lead any group I was a part of, and this group was no different. My mission was not to be just another voice at the table so that I could have a slice of pizza. If I was going to spend my time with these folks, then we were going to win something. The only reason I announced my intention to the group so blatantly was because I wanted them to not be surprised when I was the only voice giving commands and direction.

The team needed direction and they were willing to give this pushy new kid a chance. I recruited more kids to the robotics team daily, and would place everyone into small groups focused on only one task. When it came to integrating two systems onto the same platform, I would have my smaller group leaders work together. I was able to learn a little bit from every group as I moved around the room and visited all of my teams, such as the structures team, programming team, pneumatics systems team, electrical systems team, and outreach team. Some of my peers had no desire to work directly on robots, so I found them a job creating websites or allowed them to utilize their sewing skills to make the robot more stylish. Mr. Reis and many of the other teacher volunteers were very hands-off, so I was virtually unchallenged. Building these robots was giving me everything I needed. *FIRST* was about more than robots. The robots were a vehicle for me to learn important life skills. I came in not knowing what to expect—of the program or of myself. I left with a sense that I could create my own future.

All the team improvements happened smoothly and quickly. There was only one problem: the more my team grew, the less pizza there would be to share.

# Chapter 12
## The Place

AS DR. RAMSEY had advised me, it was now time to play surrogate father to my little brother Kumasi. This meant moving in with him and my mother in their current homeless shelter. Dr. Ramsey personally drove me across town to where they were staying. I had the feeling he drove me to make sure I didn't take a detour. But I had already committed myself.

We arrived at a large white building off Lankershim in North Hollywood—*the place*. I gave Dr. Ramsey some dap and exited the car feeling like the opposite of Will Smith in the TV show *The Fresh Prince of Bel-Air*. "Hey, Doc," I yelled before Dr. Ramsey could pull away. "Go home, smell you later!"

I opened a heavy, rusty gate to walk into a relatively clean campus that had a freshly paved concrete path. When I entered the building, I was greeted by my mom's warm smile.

"Hi, Mom," I said in the most excited voice I could muster. She greeted me with a hug and a kiss, then grabbed my hand and energetically dragged me down the hallway. She was excited to show me this new shelter.

"Every family gets their own room! No more sleeping on a cot surrounded by hundreds of people. We're moving up!"

My mother was too happy to have too little, but I decided that I would mimic her attitude. The room she brought me to was very small. It had a closet and a bathroom attached, and almost no space to move around, as the two beds in the room already brought the place to max capacity. She showed me the cafeteria area, adding, "Most nights the food is barely edible, but if a church or organization decides to come volunteer, that group will usually bump the quality up significantly."

Mom and Kumasi had lived in four different shelters in the past few months. I was trying to understand what was good about this one compared to the others.

We walked down a different hallway to the kids' activity room this time. Even though it was late in the evening, there were lots of children running through the halls. When we reached a small door with a bright glow emanating from it, I knew we were in the right place. I found Kumasi among the kids immediately, because in that moment no one else mattered. You can't hug and kiss your little brother in a room full of strangers, so I put him into a headlock and squeezed him to prove that I loved and missed him.

When I finally let go, Kumasi introduced me to some kids and showed me activities: the room offered video games, board games, computers, and arts and crafts. But my eye was drawn to a fancy piano in the back of the room. I told Kumasi that my girlfriend, Janie, had been teaching me how to play classical songs on her piano. Kumasi made some sarcastic comment about how he didn't think I had any talent. That was all I needed to hear.

"Challenge accepted, son!" I yelled at Kumasi as I sat down to the piano.

I opened up the piano, and the keys were flawless. It looked as if no one had ever played it. I cleared my throat and told people I was going to play. Most of them ignored me or just shrugged.

The sound from this piano was deep and rich as I serenaded the crowd with a melody. I knew Kumasi must have been in shock, because I had never explained to him just how good of a pianist my instructor was. None of my stories about Janie were embellished, I just never finished telling them in any great detail.

As I performed, people stopped talking and gathered around me. More people heard the piano and came streaming through the door. Others hung out in the hall to listen to the mini-concert. Or peered in to figure out who was playing.

"Does anyone know the name of that song?" I asked.

"I think that was Beethoven!" one of the little girls screamed across the room.

"You are right! I just played Ludwig von Beethoven's 'Fur Elise'!"

People crowded closer and shook my hand. I must have met everyone in the shelter that night. My mom and Kumasi were elated at the welcome I was receiving. I guess I lived up to whatever hype they gave these folks about me. My family was proud of me.

# Chapter 13
## Running with the Cool Kids

FOOTBALL WAS NOT the only way to stay busy at school. Instead of joining sophomore year, I stayed with the track and field coach. I ran on the cross-country team and got to know more athletes at Crenshaw High. I learned that cross-country drew the "cool kids." Top athletes from basketball, volleyball, and tennis signed up for cross-country. Everyone except the football team, which was in season at the time.

Unlike football, it was very odd training with this group, because practice consisted of running around the city in a big group. I wanted to question the coach's methods, because the team's colors—blue and gold—were not exactly gang neutral everywhere we ran. Surely we would find ourselves in trouble if we ran through the wrong neighborhood. A few times we got dangerously close to my old hood: the Jungles. And Bloods don't exactly like the color blue.

If we came up against problems that would cause the group to need to fight, I was ready. But the moment for me to protect all these defenseless skinny kids never came through.

These skinny kids always ate a decent meal before we started our run. I'd be in the restaurant hanging out with them before practice, but I'd never buy anything. I ain't had no money. One day my teammate Moriah Johnson approached me inside an In-N-Out Burger. He saw me sitting in the corner as everyone else ate and handed me some money. "Yohancé, go get in line and buy you something." This senior was six-foot-six, with perfect skin and that nice wavy hair all the girls liked. Moriah was supposedly the coolest and most popular guy at my school, so how did he know my name? I barely knew his name, and it was mostly because everyone always talked about how cool it was to have a celebrity at the school. Apparently, he wasn't just the captain of the basketball team, or the son of an NBA player. He was the star on his own television show, *Baldwin Hills*. And everyone had seen his popular TV show except me. I thanked Moriah and had my first In-N-Out burger that day.

## Let's Run

When it was time to compete against other schools at cross-country meets, I proved that I really wasn't a leader of the pack. I could not keep up with anyone for too long, but if a girl ahead of me had a nice butt, I could manage to run a little bit faster. There was such a grand selection of girls to chase in those meets, running three miles around the park. White girls, black girls, Latinas, and Asian chicks all zipped ahead as I struggled to maintain a decent pace.

I didn't mind getting passed or lapped by any of these pretty ladies, but I never liked to see any of my male teammates overtaking me. If they laughed at how slow I was running, I'd give them a little shoulder charge or try to block them. If there were no girls to gawk at, I would dick around with any guy who passed me.

"Dude, get out of my way! This isn't football!" Rodney once shouted at me.

The coaches and referees never saw my shenanigans, though, because there were just too many blind spots in the winding hills along the route. Whenever I was out of sight, I would either start walking or look for someone new to mess with. I would let my imagination run wild, acting like some type of roadside bandit—like Swiper from *Dora, the Explorer*.

I had too much thinking time on my hands while running, and I started thinking that maybe cross-country was a bad choice. Was I on the right vector? I enjoyed being aggressive and chasing girls, so why wasn't I dedicating my time to pursuing these things more directly? Why wasn't I honing these skills in real life, instead of pursuing them metaphorically on the cross-country team? I was investing energy into trying to get to the end of this race—even though the finish line held no prize I wanted.

My struggle against the current made no sense anymore. I didn't want to be homeless, broke, dirty, or hungry when everything in this world felt like it could be mine for the taking. All I had to do was shake off this sense of integrity; I felt I was being held back by character. How about if I became the best worst version of myself? All I had to do was make up my mind that the most important thing in this universe was me.

I was only a few seconds away from making this dramatic change in my life when someone bumped into me and nearly sent me to the ground. He barely knew me, so why was he acting so friendly to me all of a sudden?

Moriah Johnson had just run by and shoulder-charged me, which made me wonder if I was going to be the one to break this pretty boy's face. This rich kid had paid for my lunch once, so did he think he owned me now?

"Yohancé, you've gotta run faster for the Shaw," Moriah said as he slowed down for me to catch up to him.

"What do you mean, the Shaw?"

"The Shaw, Yohancé! The Shaw! Crenshaw! You're wearing school colors, but you ain't doing shit to earn them. You walkin' out here, and that shit ain't coo."

"I get it, I think. I'll run with ya then."

"Good. Keep up as long as you can, even if you fall behind. Don't stop until you pass the finish line. Do it for the Shaw."

I could not keep up with Moriah for long, but his words set me straight. After his pep talk, I maintained my fastest pace yet. I had real motivation now, and not just a fleeting sense of lust or mischief driving me. He'd bumped into me at the most opportune time and motivated me to finish more than this one race.

I wanted to compete against him now, to be like Moriah. In that moment, I remembered the speech The Rock gave me that pushed me away from drugs, gangs, and forward in life. Moriah had provided a fresh reminder of that same message.

There was a different path I could take. I could become a more positive role model in my community and say no to this cycle of drugs, gangs, and violence. That path would just be a little harder to take, but well worth it.

# Chapter 14
## Twice, Fighting the Wrong Enemy

KEEPING A POSITIVE attitude proved to be very challenging while living with my family in the shelter. Convincing Kumasi to do the same was even harder. He was not a small child whose imagination I could foster into conjuring a new reality. If I told him that things were better than they really were, he would simply call me a liar. I lied a lot in those days. If the bread being served was soggy, and the corn had a funny taste to it, I lied. I would tell him that everything was delicious. When I couldn't afford to buy everyone a meal, and I only brought enough for my mom and Kumasi to eat, I lied. I told them I had already eaten and that they were only getting my scraps and leftovers. If our mother woke us up in the middle of the night with another one of her episodes, I lied. I said it was my fault because I left the TV on, so I'd try and make the commotion go away somehow.

In that winter of 2009, my patience with my family and shelter life seemed infinite, until it wasn't. On most weekends a line of kids wanted to play videogames in the main recreational room. In order to avoid this line and keep Kumasi busy, I frequently bought, borrowed, or somehow acquired the latest videogames for him to play. We had a little videogame set-up in the room that my family shared. I would take a break from playing classical music or studying to play videogames as well. Kumasi and I had a system in place for sharing time on the console. If one of us died in a game, or lost in a major way, our turn was over. When it was my turn to play, I usually would pass on my turn and allow Kumasi to continue to play. This cycle became the norm after a while, and Kumasi realized I was not even paying attention, so he stopped asking me if I wanted my turn.

"How many times have you skipped my turn now?"

"I forgot how many times. You have to wait until I die again to play now."

I had just finished another paper for school, and I needed a break from staring at my phone. Instead of waiting for my turn, I snatched the controller out of Kumasi's hand.

"My turn!" I said with a smirk as I made Kumai's video game character jump off a cliff and die. I thought my move was hilarious until Kumasi punched me in the mouth. I thought Kumasi must have lost his mind. My little brother was an inch or two taller than me, but he was very skinny and had a fraction of the strength that I possessed. I was fifteen years old, but I had the body of a twenty-five-year-old athlete. I knew I was going to hurt this boy.

I knew I had to instill some fear in him so he would not ever try to fight me again. I balled up a fist and made some aggressive motions in his direction to make him think I was throwing a punch. I expected him to flinch and cower. Instead, Kumasi threw two punches that landed square in my chest. I set the controller down and stared at the boy in disbelief. He dodged away, but there was nowhere to run. He was cornered.

But in that moment I heard that voice in my head: *But no one will really win this fight. You both can only lose.*

I had heard my inner voice say things like this before, but never had it been so wise and mature as this. I realized that this was wrong. I was supposed to be his caregiver, his surrogate father. That was why I had moved into the shelter. So why was I ready to destroy my little brother? Kumasi was ready for my attack, but I simply turned around and walked out of the room. Kumasi could win this fight if it meant that one day we could both be winners.

I went directly to the piano after my fight with Kumasi. I knew that the emotional lump in my throat would produce some of the best music, and I needed to share this great burden before it overwhelmed me. Every key I struck on the piano that day told my story. I was not ready to tell it in words, but the music just flowed out of me. When I finished, there was a new warmth and a glow in the room that wiped away all my sadness, pain, and frustration. It was still a bright and sunny Saturday morning. And though noon was quickly approaching, there was still time to make better memories.

The folks at the shelter began wandering in as I played the piano, and soon I had a small audience. It surprised me.

I was approached by a shelter volunteer named Sarah, a blonde twenty-eight-year-old girl from the Valley. Sarah introduced me to her fellow volunteers. Both the volunteers and I felt a little awkward when I told her I was fifteen and that I lived here. But I did not let the awkwardness linger for long. People are connected to one another in deeper ways than they can imagine, so I decided to find the connection between Sarah and me. I rattled off a lot of information about my life until something stuck. I learned that her boyfriend, whom she met in a yoga class, was a science teacher at Crenshaw High. Mr. Schaefer taught Advanced Placement Chemistry and Physics. And I was in his class.

As soon as I told Sarah this fact, I realized I'd added another person at my high school to the growing list who knew I was homeless. But I felt Mr. Schaefer was someone I could trust.

My conversation with Sarah came to an end when I was told that there was a game of flag football in the park. The other kids had begged me all week to play. Even though it was only flag football, I still didn't think it was very safe for them to be on the same field as me. I could be aggressive and overly competitive in flag football. The last time I played flag football, I was in a big tournament in middle school called the Bird Bowl. My buddy Toney was on the opposite team, and I pushed him so hard that he dropped the game-winning pass. My technique of grabbing people before snatching their flags off would look like a tackle—and tackling was not allowed in flag football. The ages and sizes of many of the kids in the shelter made me not want to play even more. I felt like a man among boys, even though a few of them were older than me. In the end, however, the group won me over, and I decided I would play.

For most of the game I played quarterback. I allowed everyone to run around and I would just pass people the ball. I figured that as long as they were all far away from me, no one would get hurt. Kumasi was smart enough to avoid the game entirely. He gave several of the boys warnings about me, but they still wanted me to play.

One of the eldest boys annoyed me by picking on some of the younger players on my team. If I tossed the ball to one of the little girls, I expected everyone to at least let her run down the field a bit before snatching her flags off. Instead, this boy would showboat and tease the players on my team as he ran circles around them. He was fifteen, and he thought he was a hot shot because he could shut down an eight-year-old girl in flag football. He was leading his team to a victory, while I was holding myself back for fear that I would hurt him or the other bigger kids on his team.

There was one little boy on my team who, I felt, did not get the ball enough. I would try to pass the ball to him, but he would always drop it, or my throw would be off and he'd be unable to catch it. My solution was to have him run all the way to the end zone, and when he was far enough to where people thought I could not reach him, I would launch him the ball. I figured no one was expecting this play. The throw was perfect, but when the ball finally came down, it landed in the wrong set of hands. The showboating fifteen-year-old had intercepted my pass. I immediately zoomed down the field, past my teammates who stood in shock. I was going to stop him from gaining any more yards on this play by snatching his flags off right where he stood.

My biggest mistake that day was forgetting to slow down before I confronted this boy. As my full momentum slammed into him, I watched this boy fly backward and land flat on his back. He was still breathing, and tears were seeping from his eyes. It took a while for him to get up off the ground, and there seemed to be no permanent damage. I felt horrible for what I had done to him, but my remorse was not enough for this boy's older brother. He began yelling at me for picking on someone so much smaller than myself, even though his brother and I were the same age. The older brother was seventeen. He started to call me names and shove me. It began to really annoy me, since this was the second time today someone was picking a fight with me.

I could not bring myself to actually strike the older brother. I had passed up a fight against Kumasi for the greater good—despite how much I loved to fight. So why couldn't I do it again for this boy? We were all homeless, every single kid on this field. If we got into a big fight, then all our families could be kicked out of the shelter. The enemy was poverty, hunger, and scarcity, not each other. In that moment I most wanted nothing more than to bash that boy's head in, but I reflected on the wisdom I had given myself earlier that day: *But no one will really win this fight. You both can only lose.*

I walked off the field that day, even as that boy continued to call me names and make jokes about my crazy momma. I was not going to let him turn me into a real loser.

# Chapter 15
## A Real Job Interview

SUMMER BREAK WAS quickly approaching, and I needed to find some sort of activity to occupy my time. Mostly I wanted to find a job, but I was willing to participate in any program that could provide me with a meal every day. Summer school was not an option for me, because none of the more advanced courses I needed were offered at Crenshaw for the summer. I knew that the tail end of the summer would be filled with football practice, because my hiatus was over. I was going back to playing football for Crenshaw High the start of my junior year.

I was accepted into a Robotics course and a Statistics course at the University of California in Los Angeles (UCLA) for the summer. The program only lasted a few weeks, so I had to find another opportunity that would last at least a month. I thought about working a small part-time summer job, but I remember wanting something more than just a paycheck.

Tim Wright volunteered at my high school as a coach on the robotics team. He looked like a young nerdy version of Santa Claus. He always had a smile on his face and a handkerchief in his breast pocket to wipe his glasses as he told a story. Tim was an engineer at a large aerospace company and told me that I could work with him. I thought he was joking. Why would one of the biggest engineering companies in the country hire a fifteen-year-old for the summer? Tim explained that his company regularly hired college students every summer for internships. Although I wasn't in college, there was work for me.

Tim insisted that the leadership and technical skills I'd fostered on the robotics team would directly transfer to working as an engineer for the summer. He told me that I was mature enough and more than capable of getting the job. But the more Tim explained the job, the further away from reality the whole thing sounded. In order to qualify, I had to take several health exams, get a background check, obtain a secret government clearance, and run through a fire storm of red tape. The whole process seemed hard enough, but to top it all off, I had to convince a whole team of senior engineers to hire me instead of the many college students from Stanford and MIT who applied every year. So all I had to do was make the impossible happen.

The Aerospace Corporation hosts a huge science fair every year where they invite local high schools in Los Angeles to their campus. Every school does a presentation of a school-wide project and also receives a tour of the various laboratories and facilities. Tim Wright secured Crenshaw's robotics team a last-minute invite to present at the event. We scrambled to set up our station alongside the other schools and showed off our 115-pound robot that could play soccer. But I was distracted by the idea that this was a preliminary job interview; I had the opportunity to discuss the robot to every senior engineer in the company. As the captain of the team, I was uniquely qualified to explain all the systems involved, though I still had my systems leaders ready to back me up should I misspeak.

Walking onto the company campus was an education. The place was so pristine and full of brain power. Every monument positioned around the campus was an academic lesson; the giant burned-up hunks of metal were old satellites, or rockets, that were now placed on massive stone displays. The Aerospace courtyard was humongous, with some beautiful and unique architecture.

The engineers seemed very engaged as they walked from station to station, asking questions of all the students. I was never sure if I was potentially talking to my future boss, so I gave everyone an extensive presentation of our robot. Tim Wright was rounding up all the senior engineers to bring to our station, and the only adult at the station was the team director, Mr. Reis.

"I used ta wurk fur a company dis big, Yohancé," he chattered between senior engineer visits. "We built helicopters, ya. Boy dem were de days." Mr. Reis always had a good story to tell.

Tim would periodically come back with a new engineer.

"Yohancé, this is Alonzo Prator," Tim said with his St. Nick smile. "He's the director of the satellite energy systems and space batteries test group in laboratory six. You need to give him the best presentation."

Alonzo was a mature gentleman in his early sixties, bald, black, and a top-class engineer. He had a lot of energy. He was about six-foot-three, but he was frequently doubled over laughing hysterically. I knew this man's personality type very well. He was an old-school cat, with a love for life and a desire to enjoy every second of it. I knew exactly how to convince him to hire me. Like everyone at the event, he was a nerd. I had to show him that I was one, too. But first, I had to put on display my exuberant go-getter attitude. Alonzo needed to hear a few jokes sprinkled into my conversations about populating an integrated circuit. Luckily, none of my presentation felt forced or fake. I was simply being my absolute self, and it was working.

At the end of my presentation, Tim asked Alonzo if he would consider hiring me for the summer to work in his laboratory. I watched a look of frustration stretch across Alonzo's face as he contemplated the task of hiring a high school student. Alonzo then made a speech that was becoming very familiar to me: "I can't promise you anything, but let me get back to you."

But these weren't just excuses; Alonzo promised to go back to his laboratory and speak with the rest of the team leaders. If they gave him the OK, then he could give me a formal interview that same day.

I was tempted to give Tim Wight a high-five as we watched Alonzo cheerfully skip and two-step back to his lab. Instead, I lifted Tim into the air with a forceful bear hug, even though his big belly meant it took all my strength to pick him up.

I didn't have the job yet, but even getting this far was a cause for celebration. I turned to the rest of my team and said that if I got a job as a lab technician at the Aerospace Corporation, I would pave the road for them to get one too. We would all accomplish the impossible.

It was around lunch time when Alonzo asked to meet with me for an interview. Tim Wright and Mr. Reis pulled me into a corner to give me two lifetimes' worth of interview coaching in less than thirty minutes. Tim was talking about the importance of eye contact, while Mr. Reis was trying to brush any dust off my shirt. They switched roles, and Tim remade the collar on my shirt while Mr. Reis taught me to smile if my boss's joke wasn't funny, and to laugh if it was even slightly humorous. If I wasn't ready before, this last-minute boot camp surely kicked me into gear.

Alonzo walked into the company cafeteria and beckoned for me to join him at a back table. He was carrying a thick folder. This time around, Alonzo was not as easygoing as when I had met him earlier. He was not telling jokes, or smiling. He was trying to figure out if I was going to embarrass him and the company. His interview questions were not easy, and I found myself bluffing my answers often.

Halfway through the interview, Alonzo asked, "What makes you think that I can convince the board of this company to allow me to hire a fifteen-year-old boy from South Central Los Angeles? A boy from Crenshaw, no less?"

In my mind I thought, *I have no chance of getting this job.* Instead, I pushed away the negative thinking, looked Alonzo square in the eye, and spoke in a low but steady tone. I was speaking from a mature and confident place in my soul, using words that seemed strange even to me.

"Alonzo. They are going to laugh at your recommendation, but be unperturbed by their ignorance. When you have their attention once more, you will impress upon them that this young man is in no way equal to any fifteen-year-old they have ever, or will ever, meet in their life. You will speak volumes on my character, and my sense of purpose. Ultimately, I will pay back this company with great distinction for taking the chance of hiring me. You just have to convince the board to get out of their own way."

I think I used the right combination of words, because my speech unlocked Alonzo's smile. He was grinning from ear to ear, and he let out a triumphant laugh. Alonzo told me I had passed the interview, but now it was time for me to jump through a thousand hoops to get qualified to work in the defense industry. Then he dumped the contents of the large folder out, spilling onto the table lots of documents for me to review and sign.

"Yohancé, you work on making all these appointments and filling out this mountain of paperwork, and I will work on getting the board to allow me to hire you this summer."

I didn't need to ask about salary or how hard the job would be. I already knew it was the best deal anyone had ever given me.

# Chapter 16
## The Bus and the Train

THURSDAYS WERE ALWAYS the lightest days of practice for track and field. Friday was the big track meet, and no one wanted to get injured before they competed. My buddy Prince Horne and I had garnered something of a reputation for taking Thursdays even lighter than coach intended. Instead of jogging a mile or two around the track, we would spend most of the short practice stretching and lying out in the sun. It was May 6, 2009, and the beautiful spring Los Angeles weather was perfect for a lazy track and field practice.

At the end of practice, Prince asked me if I wanted to go get some burgers and hang out. Normally I would have to decline because I never had money in my pocket, but that day I had a pocket full of food stamps. My mother had just put me in charge of the family's EBT (Eat Better Today!) card, the government food assistance program we qualified for. When it came to buying food, I was rich. So I took Prince up on his offer.

We sat down at the local McDonald's and tore into a few dollar menu burgers as we discussed next year's football season for our high school.

"They got no idea how lucky they are that you and me are joining the team this year, Yohancé!" said Prince. He made me feel like we were some sort of secret weapons. Neither of us had played football for Crenshaw High School the previous year due to family issues. Prince's mother needed him to take care of her as her health declined. But she recovered enough that Prince decided to go back to the game he loved. I don't think I ever confessed to

Prince that I did not play football sophomore year because I was homeless. But eventually I figured out the public transportation schedule between the field and the shelter. Two busses and two trains, involving two and a half hours of travel time, were what it took for me to cross the city. Not easy, but worth it.

Once Prince and I said our goodbyes and left the burger joint, I started my transition into what I call my traveler's persona. Generally I have a smile on my face and am very approachable, but all that had to change when I stepped onto the bus in South Central LA. I had to look unapproachable. Hard. Not an easy target. I had to become someone I would never want to talk to or mess with. These are the traits you want to have as a passenger on these buses. After many years of riding the bus, I thought I had perfected a technique to give off exactly this perception.

But that afternoon, a woman boarded the bus. Instead of shying away from the big buff black guy with the chip on his shoulder, she decided to sit right next to me.

*I can't believe how good she smells! Look at her hair and her sundress and, oh my God, she is beautiful!*

At that point I had to plug into my self-discipline, my character and values. It would be better if I remained stoic and unapproachable. Besides, I already had a girlfriend. The bus had about an hour left in its route and I had to ride this thing until the end of the line. Surely, I thought, this temptation would be brief. Because she was sure to get up, move seats, or exit the bus soon.

But she didn't.

"End of the Line! Welcome to Hollywood! Hollywood and Vine, folks!" shouted the bus driver.

We had not spoken or interacted at this point. This whole experience could go down as just a cool story to tell a few buddies at the track meet tomorrow.

*Prince, yesterday I sat next to the most beautiful woman in the world on a bus to Hollywood.*

Details started to rush into my mind of how I would tell the story as I stood up to exit the bus. There was a long line of passengers heading for the front door, the only exit. I could still smell her perfume as she stood behind me in line. It was strong, but not overpowering. I was almost out of the front door when my fantasies and daydreaming about telling the story came to a screeching halt.

"You know you don't have to look so angry, right?"

*She spoke to me.*

I turned around as my foot landed on the sidewalk to reply to her. I was trying to get a good look at her—something I couldn't do when she was sitting next to me. I guess it was more of a feeling and a few short glimpses that convinced me that I was sitting next to a goddess. When I saw her up close and face to face, I thought my heart might stop beating. She had long, flowing hair, a sort of golden complexion you rarely see except in movies, and the most symmetrical, prettiest facial features ever.

It was time to respond to her comment about being angry. All I could muster was a smile as I said, "Sorry."

She giggled and asked me where I was headed. As I was about to answer, she interrupted me.

"I really like your body, by the way."

It was the sweetest interruption I had ever known.

I thanked her and told her I had to catch the train to go an hour or so north of Hollywood.

"I'll walk with you to the train station. It's only a block or two away, right?" she said. She told me her name was Rachel, she was twenty-two years old, and she had just moved out of her parents' house and come to Hollywood.

I told her I was only fifteen and that my name rhymes with Beyoncé, etc., etc. Rachel did not believe that I was only fifteen. She thought I was twenty-five and told me so until I showed her my Crenshaw High School identification card.

We walked to the subway station while I told her about my ambitions to get good grades, do well in sports, and go to a good college. She planned to become a movie star and knew her outgoing personality would get her there. She waited with me at the platform for the subway, which took a long time to show up. The whole time she never stopped complimenting my looks. It was as if Rachel was somehow more attracted to me then I was to her, which I thought was impossible. She wanted to feel on my shoulders and arms, and even marveled at the shape of my backside and calves. Repeatedly. I felt a bit weird at the time, but she convinced me that this is just how older women act when they know what they want.

Eventually my train showed up, and I thought that my time with this beautiful woman had come to an end. She was smart, funny, outgoing, and probably the most good-looking person I would ever have a conversation with. But I already had a girlfriend and a place I had to be. If I did not get back to the shelter in time, I could miss my meal at the soup kitchen. The only reason my muscles were that big in the first place was because if I could help it, I didn't miss meals—or gym time.

When I stepped toward the train, Rachel grabbed my hand. She asked if I could catch the next train instead. I told her yes, I could chat a while longer. She didn't let go of my hand, though. Rachel asked me if I would come to her apartment with her. I tried to play dumb and ask why and what for, but she saw straight through me playing coy.

"You don't want to cheat on your girlfriend," Rachel said. "I see that, but I know you are just playing dumb right now. Besides, this would not be your first time having sex."

She was right.

I tried to find every excuse not to go with her to her apartment, though. I searched my brain, and all I found was an Olympic Coliseum full of men shouting profusely at me. It was as if I was a gladiator in the center of the Coliseum and everyone was yelling at me: *Go! Do it! What are you waiting for?*

I wasn't the kind of guy to make impulsive decisions, though. And I was a suspicious person, so I thought long and hard. What if this whole thing was a set-up, and Rachel had some friends at her apartment, ready to beat me up? Well, I already said I was poor and homeless, so robbing me was not worth it. Also, I am an extremely good fighter. If there were people waiting to beat me up, I could win. Dinner at the shelter could wait. I followed Rachel home.

# Chapter 17
## Jimmy's Terrible, Terrible Advice

PEOPLE USUALLY HATE interludes, but I am going to have to ask you to trust me on this one—it's necessary. I want to take you forwards and backwards in the story at the same time. Backwards because I want you to re-read something; forwards because I'm taking you straight to my senior year in high school—2011. Now, I want you to go back to the very beginning of this book and re-read my poem, "Where I'm From."

Did it?

Done it?

Good. This is the chapter that explains a lot of that poem. I am sure many people will want to skip this chapter and get back to the Rachel story that everyone is raving about, but trust me, you should hear Jimmy's terrible, terrible advice first.

Rather than go line by line and explain what the poem is meant to convey, I want to tell you why I wrote it and who I wrote it for. I wrote the poem because I was tired of bowing down to the gang members in Los Angeles. The poem is for them, though I have never delivered it entirely. When I had the chance to break from the norm and answer their interrogations with my poem, I choked.

In LA, the first thing a gangbanger asks someone is, "Where you from!?" They ask this question in the most aggressive and intimidating voice they can muster. Basically, they are asking if you are a part of a rival gang, or if you will willingly consent to being robbed. If you are a part of a rival gang, then being robbed is the least of your concerns, 'cause somebody is probably getting shot. The *proper* response to this question is, "I don't bang." And if you say it with enough respect and humility, you might get away only missing a few dollars out of your pocket. I always wanted to flip the script and become the aggressor when a gangbanger asked me this. I'd daydream about yelling my poem, "Where I'm From," back at them in response. I'd snatch something of theirs and prove to them that they were messing with the wrong motherfucker. I wanted to be that crazy nigga with nothing to lose who was willing to die for the few pennies in his pocket. It was all just a crude fantasy until my friend Jimmy taught me how to fight multiple gang members at once. I knew as soon as I'd heard his advice that I would be stupid enough to try it.

Jimmy was a rather large and muscular Crenshaw teammate of mine who claimed to be an equal or better fighter than me. We traded stories of previous bouts in our lives, always trying to one up each other. Like me, he was a very happy individual with no anger problems; he just liked to throw fists.

We had a few very similar stories. In my story I had approached three Samoan brothers in the laundromat and asked them to fight me. I thought this approach was kind of unique. It turns out that Jimmy did the exact same thing to a bunch of Jamaican brothers he met at a park. As a result of these fights, we both had a great time and made some really cool friends.

In trying to compete with Jimmy's love for a good scuffle, I mentioned a few times when I had fought multiple people at one time. There was no real technique to it; I had just been put in a few bad situations.

Jimmy replied, "Yeah, that's easy. You just fight in the middle of the street where cars are coming."

I thought Jimmy's advice was radical. Who thinks of stuff like this? And does it really work? I would not have to beat up one guy until the other three or four attackers got scared. I simply had to make one of them get hit by a car and then the whole thing would be over. But what if the guy who gets hit by the car is me?

I did not think about that last question until I had already used Jimmy's advice. It worked out for me, but it most certainly will not ever work out for you. So here is how I survived another fight with multiple attackers at the same time using Jimmy's terrible, terrible advice.

It was a Friday night in the spring of 2011. It was very late as I was standing on Martin Luther King Jr. Boulevard. I had just come from a girlfriend's house where I had spent way too much time. It was almost midnight, and I still had more than two hours of buses and trains to take to get to the shelter. I was a senior in high school at this point, seventeen years old. I had recently been awarded two different scholarships for college, and I had all of the merchandise and money with me in my backpack. I remember thinking that between the books, computers, and cash held in my backpack, it was worth close to five thousand dollars.

I was standing at a poorly lit bus stop, listening to an iPod. I was a football star at this point. My team had won the city championship. But there was a problem; my blue and gold Crenshaw team colors were the same as a local gang's colors. Trouble was, I was wearing these colors in a rival gang's neighborhood.

As a champion, I had a big ego. I thought if anyone can get away with dressing as a Crip in a notorious Blood neighborhood, it was me. I did feel a little stupid standing at that really dark bus stop, looking like an easy target, but I was jamming. My music was loud and you couldn't tell me nothin'.

Three guys in dark clothing walking down the street stopped and asked me something I could not hear. I turned down my music and greeted them. They walked on by after giving me some deep looks. At this point I decided to walk a block or two down the street to the next bus stop. Something about the lights being a lot brighter—and this bus stop being located in front of a church—gave me a greater sense of safety.

Ten minutes later, there was still no bus, but the same three individuals had come back. They looked like they were my age.

They asked me, "Where you from!?"

I remember thinking, this is it. This is the time to tell them where I'm really from!

I took my earphones out and started reciting my poem slowly.

"I'm from nothing, no how, and no way. From that ruthless dog eat—"

"GIMMIE DAT!" shouted one of the gangbangers. He'd reached for my iPod, which was in the front pocket of my blue hoodie. I dodged his hand and retreated back two steps toward the edge of the sidewalk. He did not know my poem, but he sure was quick to take it over.

"Nigga, stop rapping at me and run that shit! Gimmie yo fucking iPod and tell us why the fuck you out here wearing all that flue." Bloods don't say the word blue. They say flue (to be disrespectful to a rival gang color).

I told them the normal thing I usually say. "I'm from nowhere. I don't gangbang."

That was not enough for them. They asked me the same questions again, and I paused.

I told them my name rhymes with Beyoncé, starts with a Y. Yoh-Hon-Say. And I am a football player at Crenshaw High, where our colors are blue and gold. I wasn't a Crip, I was just wearing my school colors.

The smallest of the three guys yelled at me, telling me one last time to give him my iPod. Instead, I listened to Jimmy's advice. I punched the guy, grabbed my backpack off the ground, and ran into the street. This part of Martin Luther King Jr. Boulevard had six lanes across and was incredibly busy.

As my three attackers followed me into the street, I dodged two cars. As they darted into traffic to kick my ass, one boy was sideswiped by a car and had his arm broken. I was standing in the middle of the street squared up waiting for the boy with the now broken arm to come fight. He and the other two attackers ran away rather than fight me in the middle of MLK Boulevard. I'd essentially beat up three gangbangers with one punch. I was the real life One Punch Man.

That was the last time anyone ever banged on me, so I never got the chance to finish my poem—and the ending is the best part. That's where I reveal that I believe there is some sort of purpose or meaning to my life. That's the only thing I ever pray for: that I continue to walk down the path

God wants me to. This belief is how I got to the LGMR experience (see Chapter 19).

I thought to myself, *God must want me to go through this,* so I just said fuck it, and let Rachel lead me to her apartment.

# Chapter 18
# Rachel's Apartment

IT WAS MAY 6, 2009, a bright and beautiful day in Los Angeles. And I had just met someone new.

"Your hands are really sweaty, Yohancé," said Rachel.

"I know, I know. You can understand why I am a bit nervous though, right?" I said, trying to stay cool.

We had been holding hands since we left the train station, and my heart was beating so loudly I thought it could stop traffic. Hollywood is a very busy tourist area and people were staring at me, many guys giving me a high-five with their eyes, thinking I had a celebrity on my arm. That's how drop-dead sexy she was.

Rachel assured me her place was a couple blocks away, and that I had no reason to be nervous. She asked me if this was the first time I had been offered sex from someone I had just met. I told her no one will ever believe this story because shit like this does not happen to people in real life. Especially with women that look like her. She chuckled and declared that I had just not met more mature women yet, and that this sort of thing would definitely be a part of my future. I was nervous and a bit paranoid about the whole situation, but my feet continued moving me forward.

When we reached her apartment, I was relieved to find that there was not a group of men waiting to bash my head in. I felt so good that I fell backward onto the soft bed in the middle of the room. I lay there laughing as Rachel sat in a chair and took off her shoes. I let her know that I was still in disbelief about what was about to happen between us.

Rachel started crawling from her chair to the foot of the bed where I was laying down. I tried to sit up, but she pushed me back down and told me to relax. She pulled my shorts down slowly as she rubbed on my stomach and my legs. I removed my shirt quickly, but she gestured for me to slow down. As she played with my underwear I ran my fingers through her hair. Somehow I'd missed the fact that she had braces, and now that she was ready to go down on me, this small detail made my dick harder than it'd ever been before. I told her I like to be sucked really fast and really deep. When she saw my penis, she smiled really widely and said she knew I wouldn't disappoint her. She started off really slowly, licking just the tip, which made me think she did not know how to suck dick. I started to think that maybe all beautiful women do not know how to suck dick. I told her to go a little bit faster. A little bit deeper. She was soon getting the hang of it and really started getting into it.

*This is heaven,* I thought to myself; I will never feel more success, accomplishment, joy, or happiness than what I feel now as this woman performs fellatio on me.

She stopped sucking my dick after only ten minutes and told me to flip over. But I told her no, and that if she was taking a break, then I wanted to watch her undress. She did a little bit of a striptease for me, but I didn't get to see everything I wanted to. Her breasts were perfect—not too big, not too small. She had them Goldilocks titties, and they were real as far as I could tell. She looked so good naked that it felt like I was in a dream. The hairs above her vagina were trimmed and neat, but not bald—I liked that. I reached down to touch her vagina and she caught my hand. Rachel asked me if I had truly ever been with a woman. I told her yes, but never someone as beautiful as her. She placed my hands on her breasts and told me to lay back down. Break time was over.

After a few minutes more of sucking my dick, she told me to turn over, so I did. Rachel told me to grab the bed pillows and put my head face-down in them. I did as she asked, and then turned my head to look at her. She told me to stop peeking and sounded a little frustrated. I turned over, and Rachel walked across the room and opened the top drawer to her dresser. She was now holding a bottle of lotion as she walked back to the bed.

"Please stop turning around so much, Yohancé. You are messing up my fetish," Rachel said.

She explained to me that she wanted to put lotion all over my butt and play with my asshole. I told her that she was extremely weird and that I was uncomfortable. She was insistent; she had already sucked my dick and the least I could do was let her play with my ass. Then I remembered on the subway how Rachel had been complimenting me on how round my ass was. I lay face down again and felt her apply a very generous amount of lotion to my asshole. Her fingering my asshole in a pool of lotion made me feel wrong, and I asked her again if we could do something else. I did not want her playing in my asshole anymore, but it seemed to be the only thing she wanted to do. Eventually she started jerking me off at the same time, which made things a little bit better.

I started turning around abruptly to see what she was doing, but I could never catch her. I thought she was preparing to ambush me with some sex toy, but I never saw it. Each time I would flip over to look, she would aggressively flip me back over and tell me to stop it. Eventually I got accustomed to her fingers being down there, and just let it happen. She started to grind on me from behind. But something different was happening down there. I could not quite describe it at first. I knew by now what her fingers felt like, but this was not a finger. It felt bigger, warm, and slimy. She started to thrust on me more aggressively, and I panicked.

"Rachel, I'm not sure what's going on. Can you stop!?"

She groaned and complained, not wanting to stop. We were finally doing exactly what Rachel wanted. We were doing her fetish.

The whole situation confused me.

I asked Rachel what was happening. I had to know. Was I having sex with someone with two sets of genitals, or had she been using a strap-on? I told her that if it was a penis then we needed to use a condom. I asked her if she had any. I was in fear for my life, and I knew I had to play along until I got my opportunity. She stopped, pissed off, and wearily pointed to the top drawer in the dresser.

"Fine," she sighed, "grab a condom from there."

I said OK, then pulled up my shorts and walked toward the dresser. But I never opened that drawer. I grabbed my backpack, shirt, shoes, and wallet and flew out of that apartment.

As I walked briskly down the long hallway, Rachel raced to her doorway. She popped her head out and called to me mockingly, "Yohancé, just so you know—that was my dick inside you!"

# Chapter 19
## LGMR (Lust Got Me Raped)

—I am, and have always been my own biggest cheerleader

FUNNY-LOOKING STARS is all I could see as I walked back to the train station in Hollywood.

*Keep your head up, Yohancé!*

That's all I could hear, a really loud voice in my head trying to make me stop staring down at the ground. Maybe I needed to wander the streets, get tough, and do something crazy before I went back to the shelter. A bullet, a car crash, a bridge, or a drug—maybe I needed one of these in my life at this moment.

Those were the thoughts crowding my head as I boarded the train. It was late in the evening now, and there were plenty of open seats. But I stood and held onto the pole.

I could still feel the globs of lotion in my butt, and I could not imagine sitting down right now.

I felt so dirty. I felt so nasty. I felt so stupid.

No tears though. I don't think I fully understood my situation at this point. But it wasn't time to analyze, it was time to get to a safe place. That loud voice in my head just continued to bark instructions at me, and I listened the best I could.

*Open the door, Yohancé!*

I walked into the shelter, greeted my mother and little brother quickly—
and went straight to the showers.

*Wash your ass, Yohancé! Now you may cry, Yohancé.*

I took the longest shower of my life that day. I must have scrubbed
myself too hard, though, because I was bleeding in places that I thought
I ought not be. I dried off, changed clothes, and sat in an empty room
waiting for my brother and mother to leave the common areas for the
night.

*Call Mr. Johnson. Tell him what happened, Yohancé.*

"Fuck You!" I told the voice in my head. I did not want to listen anymore. I did not want to call my high school Life Skills teacher right now. I
was still getting over the fact that I just got raped.

The questions kept echoing in my head:

*Was it even rape?*

*Was it all my fault?*

*Am I gay now?*

*What would Mr. Johnson say?*

And the inner voice kept speaking to me, telling me to call Mr. Johnson.
If that was really my voice of reason, then where was this voice when I was
searching for guidance in the train station? Why was it so quiet when all the
screams of lust filled my head? Why didn't it tell me to get away from Rachel
and not follow her home?

I felt like I couldn't trust this voice anymore, because when I needed it
the most, it had abandoned me.

But then it dawned on me that the only reason I had made it safely back
to *the place* was because of the voice's guidance. That whole trip I felt like I
was blind, and I'd forgotten how to take a bus, how to walk, or how to
breathe. That voice was there when I needed it the most, and it had saved my
life.

I picked up my phone and called Mr. Johnson, even though I'd never
called him before. Part of me hoped he wouldn't pick up the phone. But he
did. And he told me to say what I needed to tell him. No matter what it was.

Mr. Johnson listened to the whole story. He told me he would come to
see me. He also insisted I call the police. I gave him my address, and he said
that he would be there as fast as humanly possible. It's about a two-hour

drive, but he showed up in less than an hour. The police arrived at the same time, and Mr. Johnson stood by my side as I gave a statement to the police. I was surprised when the officers told me to hop in the car with them. I asked what for, and they replied that we were going to get this person tonight.

*Call Dr. Ramsey, Yohancé.*

It was my inner voice again.

"Mr. Officer, I need to make another phone call first. I won't be long."

"Better hurry, young man. We don't want to miss our window of opportunity."

Dr. Ramsey was initially puzzled by my late call, and I was confused about what to tell him. It all just tumbled out.

"Doc, I need to let you know something; I was just raped by a transgender person. The cops are here; we are going to go find the person now. They are getting me a rape kit soon. And I'm OK."

I blurted the whole statement out as fast as I could, and almost hung up the phone before Dr. Ramsey could reply. He was furious. I could hear him breaking things in his house as he kept his voice low and calm over the phone. He wanted to know why I called the cops instead of him first. He said we could have handled the situation much differently, but that he was grateful that I was getting help. Dr. Ramsey said he would come to get me, but I explained that I had to go with the cops. I thanked him and hung up.

We drove up to the apartment building. We were backed by about a dozen police cars, and I told them every detail they needed to find Rachel. The officers emerged from the apartment building a few minutes later with a person in handcuffs. I told the officer in the car with me that they had the right person. He nodded and said that my description of Rachel was so detailed down to every little scar and tattoo that my visual verification was more of a formality. We left the scene and went to a hospital for the rape kit.

A rape kit consists of a bunch of tests, swabs, shots, and pictures to collect evidence about a rape. Most of the time victims have already showered before the kit, which makes it less effective. There is also a psychiatric evaluation, which is really helpful. Lying on that cold hospital table and having the doctor use a magnifying glass to pick Rachel's hair out of my pubic hair was mortifying. The doctors were all very kind, but I did not want anyone to see or touch my body until I had showered at least ten more times. When the process was over, it was very early in the morning. They gave me a new set of clothes and sent me home.

Mr. Johnson had seen me through this long and terrible process, sleep-deprived like me. And yet when I got back to the shelter, he was ready to rock—whatever I needed, say the word, he told me. He and Dr. Ramsey had been floating around the background all night, patiently and delicately trying to help my mother and little brother process what was going on.

I told Mr. Johnson that I had to go to school that day, since there was a big track meet. I attended all my regular classes like the previous day never happened. But that was hard to do, since a few times I was pulled out of class for meetings with the school nurse, school psychologist, and a police officer. But for the most part, it was a normal day.

I was at my locker between classes, grabbing a few books for my next class, when my buddy Leon walked over to me. He had a big grin on his face and was followed by this detective lady with this huge gun on her hip. I couldn't tell if the huge gun on her hip made her look small, or if she was just so small she made the gun look huge. She didn't even need a badge. That gun said everything that needed to be said. Leon looked like he'd found Waldo the way he pointed me out to this detective.

"Iiight then, Yohancé. Imma catch you later at the track meet, right?" said Leon.

"Bet. I see you later," I replied. I think Leon was just trying to make sure he didn't snitch on me. It's kind of weird to just tell the cops where another black man is—*oh yeah, he's over here, Officer.* But I think the detective lady must have convinced Leon that I was not in trouble.

Detective Sanchez introduced herself, reassured me that it was OK if I was late to class, and said she had a few questions for me. Remember, she arrived after I'd already had meetings with the nurse, psychologist, and a cop. So I was over it by now.

"Detective, I've given this story like twenty times already," I grumbled, "and the fifty thousand questions are starting to get excessive. Its's borderline harassment at this point."

"I understand, Yohancé, but this one is a little different. I need to ask you if you are willing to testify in court against umm … the person." She was speaking in code because people were still scurrying around to their classrooms. And even though they acted like they were paying us no attention, Crenshaw Cougars could hear gossip from miles away.

"Yeah, I think I can do that, Detective. Just make sure to shoot me the location, date, and time, and I will be there," I retorted. Detective Sanchez looked at me for a minute and seemed irked.

"Yohancé, if this case goes to trial, then you will have to retell your story in front of a jury. And you will have to convince them that this thing happened exactly the way you say it did."

"Yeah, I get that. This will be easy."

"No, Yohancé, you don't get it. If you don't convince the jury beyond a reasonable doubt, then this person walks away free of charge."

"I understand, but I'm really good at convincing people. Especially when it's the truth. I got this."

Detective Sanchez lowered her voice and leaned in closer.

"Yohancé, I'm trying to tell you that convincing a jury of … That someone as big and strong as you could have been *taken advantage of*, will be very difficult, if not impossible. This whole case is very different. Do things like this happen to you often? Do women often walk up to you in the street and just offer you sex?"

I could tell Detective Sanchez was trying to help me, giving me a taste of the questions the defense attorney would be asking.

"Detective Sanchez, I think I understand now. Maybe I don't want to rehash this story in a room full of strangers, and I am just acting brave right now. This whole thing is very weird for me too."

I think I gave the detective exactly what she wanted, because the conversation ended shortly after I started agreeing with her. Detective Sanchez wanted to know if she could offer Rachel a plea deal and skip taking the case to trial. I had to let that argument go, as I was focused on more important things—like this track meet coming up.

At the last minute, I decided not to compete. It just seemed like the smart thing to do. The voice in my head kept telling me to take it easy, and I finally decided to start listening again. I was still on the field cheering on every one of my Crenshaw Cougars as they passed the finish line. I never got to tell my buddy Prince the story of sitting next to the most beautiful woman on a bus to Hollywood. But I was there to hand him a water and a fist bump as he smoked everyone on the track.

# Chapter 20
## Sharing My Regrets

I FELT I had told enough people about getting raped. But my inner voice had other ideas.

*Sharing your story can only make you stronger, Yohancé.*

My inner voice seldom gave me an easy task. Who else did I need to share this story with? Maybe I needed to tell it to someone my own age. I shot that idea down very quickly. I thought there was nothing to be gained by telling another high school student. Maybe I needed to tell someone who knew me in a very different way than those whom I'd already confided in. The list of people who knew what happened that day was very short, and mostly included my male mentors. My mom was the only woman who knew. Maybe it was time for me to tell another woman—but who?

It had to be someone who could help me. I wanted to be tougher from sharing my story, and not be looked down upon like a victim. Ultimately, the person I decided to add to this circle was my girlfriend, Janie. I knew that she loved me and would allow me to be vulnerable around her. What I didn't know was how she would react to me cheating on her. I was a lying, cheating, no good, ungrateful boy pretending to be a man. But as I rode the bus for a few hours headed to Janie's house, I was determined to make a change. I was going to tell Janie the truth.

This bus ride across the city felt like the longest journey I had ever taken. Every bump in the road from potholes pushed me out of my seat. I began thinking that was a sign to get off this bus and go back to the shelter. But my inner voice persisted.

*Stay on the bus; I'm leading us somewhere, Yohancé.*

So I sat back down. There was never room for a two-way conversation with my inner voice. I received one message at a time, and mostly it sounded like me yelling at myself. So I focused on constructing a plan for how I would tell Janie that I messed up. I wanted to take responsibility and not even use the word rape. But the more I bent the story, the less I wanted to tell it to Janie. I was supposed to be telling her my truth, and here I was, trying to concoct a lie. When I stepped off the bus to walk a few city blocks up to her house, I didn't have a game plan on how I would tell her my story.

The fear and hesitation in my heart made my hand shake. I reached out to ring the doorbell to her house and then stood on the porch in a faint trance as I awaited my fate.

And then the big front door swung open.

"Yohancé! I missed you so much," Janie sighed and threw herself into my arms. "You can't go weeks at a time without coming to see me!"

I had not been avoiding her. I'd just been completely immersed in school, my activities and clubs. My incident in Hollywood had occurred only a few days ago, so our lost time together was only coincidental.

Nervous as hell, I launched into my confession. "Janie, can I tell you something?"

"No, not right now you can't. I need to show you something," she interrupted. She grabbed my hand and led me into her house. We passed through her first living room, where she had been playing one of her three pianos. I wondered what she had to show me. At least there would be some good news to offset my bad news. We entered her bedroom.

"Look how pretty it is," Janie said and gestured toward a large desk. "They love me so much, Yohancé."

Her parents had bought her a new state-of-the-art workstation that looked like it could control the entire NASA space flight program. The desk was all glass and metal, and the computers, printers, and technology hovering on it looked advanced enough to do all your work for you. I didn't know people gave gifts that where this extravagant.

We spent hours playing with the almost sci fi-like new features of her amazing home office, as I pined to exist only in this fleeting state of bliss. Before I gave her my bad news and ruined the whole day, I could be happy. I decided to steal as much happiness as I could before I told Janie my story.

"Janie, you should see how much better I've gotten on the piano. I've been practicing a lot."

"Yeah, let's go do that in a bit. First, I'm going to go to the kitchen and fix you a plate of food, though. I cooked a lot yesterday, so I'll just warm something up for you, OK?"

She kissed me on the cheek and glided out of the room before I could ask her which piano I should play.

Since it might be my last time in that house, I decided that I would play the fanciest piano she owned. That would be the big black piano in the front living room with piles of sheet music strewn across it. I thought Janie wouldn't mind, because I was no longer a novice and I could really make a piano sing. Before I could finish my warm-up, Janie had already returned with a hot plate of food. I moved off the bench and let her replace me at the piano while I ate. She was so amazing at creating beautiful music. Janie favored classical music and could string notes together that seemed impossible to play with only two hands. I focused on her hands when I watched her play. I didn't stare at her long, dark hair flowing down past her shoulders or linger on the curves of her exposed lower back. Her cropped top and tight jeans were not my focus. I wanted to see her pretty little fingers dance on those big white piano keys.

After cleaning my plate in the kitchen, I returned to the living room to find Janie continuing to play her heart out. She had stamina, and only became more intense the longer she kept at it. As she bared down on the piano keys, creating deep and passionate melodies, I came up with a bright idea of how I could help her. I was going to try to distract her from the music so she could get better at playing under pressure. Anyone can perform when they are at home in a comfortable space, but performing in less than ideal conditions is the true measure of talent.

When I cozied up to Janie from behind, she didn't even react. I put my hands on her shoulders and dropped to my knees behind her as she focused on her song. I started kissing her sides while I played with the piercing on her belly-button. She never missed a note. I slipped my right hand down inside of her tight jeans. My left hand was making a slow advance to her breasts. I could sense a small change in her musical performance, but slowly caressing her body was not enough to challenge her.

My hand was too big to fit into her tight jeans comfortably, so I took it out and unzipped the front of her pants. When I licked my fingers and stuck them inside her panties, Janie missed her first note. I wanted to lightly play with her clitoris and make her beg me for more. I pinched her nipples softly and bounced her succulent breasts in my hand to a rhythm of my own. I wanted the melody I was creating with her body to be the only one on Janie's mind.

"Yohancé, I ... I can't concentrate on the music."

"I know, Janie. I'm trying to distract you."

"That's OK. You can practice a bit now if you want."

Janie listened to me play uninterrupted for about five minutes, her hands now down my pants, then burst out, "Yohancé, you are getting really good at this!"

"Thanks! There is this piano at *the place*, that I practice on like every day. It's helping a lot."

"Yeah, I can tell. Keep playing for me, Yohancé."

If playing a really fast musical piece composed by Mozart is hard, doing so when a woman has her hands down your pants is nigh impossible. Even though I couldn't read music, I thought I was close to Janie's level when it came to talent on the piano. But she showed me just how vastly different we were. She had only missed a few notes, or briefly paused to remember where she was in the song. When it was my turn, I couldn't even spell the word "piano," much less find what note to play next. When I was finally able to compose myself and focus on the music, she pulled my dick out and started talking dirty to spite me.

"Yohancé, let me know when you wanna stop playing piano and go do a little something else."

"Janie, I didn't do this much to you. You're cheating."

"I'm just trying to make you better at playing the piano, Yohancé. Just deal with the distraction."

When I wasn't playing well, she would barely touch me. She walked her hands up and down my body like I was a piano and waited for me to get back to playing the song. If I regained my focus and started to outperform her, she'd ratchet up her attention—causing me temporary paralysis. It was a very fun game, but I knew I had no chance of winning.

When we left the piano, I felt like the happiest man alive to ever sky-dive without a parachute. Sure, I was having the time of my life now, but eventually it would all come to an abrupt ending.

*It's time to tell her, Yohancé.*

Damn that inner voice!

I felt so very evil that day, because I knew what my story might do to her. Janie struggled with depression, and even though I had a boatload of bad stories I could tell her, I usually kept them to myself. Her minor suicide attempts were a big reason why I always kept her so secret. Janie didn't embarrass me in the slightest—I loved her. I was just trying to protect her. She was always perfect, until she wasn't.

"Janie, I need to tell you something. And I need you to hear me out."

She smiled at me with glazed-over eyes that professed her feelings for me.

"Yohancé, I love you. And you can tell me anything."

Instead of holding back, I told Janie everything. Every detail poured out of me, and so did tears. She held me as I wept. I watched my sadness flood Janie's heart, and quickly it overwhelmed both of us. We cried so hard in each other's arms that I could barely finish telling the story. I was weak but determined to complete what I'd started. When I finally finished delivering every excruciating detail, I collapsed onto her lap. It was selfish of me to fall asleep, but I cried so hard that I didn't have the energy to raise my head.

When I woke up a few hours later, I was on her couch with a blanket over me. Alone. I needed to know her reaction. About the rape. About the cheating. I needed to know where Janie and I stood.

I got up and walked around the house until I found her at the new workstation. She looked up with an unsmiling face.

"Yohancé, you can't stay here tonight."

I was so happy to hear her say that to me. I had done something horrible, and I needed her to hold me accountable. I knew it was my fault. I had cracked our relationship, and it would only be a matter of time before we broke up. I took solace in knowing that I wouldn't be the cause of something happening to her. Janie was strong. She could get over me.

That was the day that I came to terms with the fact that I possessed a very flawed character. I was proud of myself for telling Janie the truth, but I was ashamed that I took my time to do it. I stole half of an incredible day that did not belong to me. If my inner voice was not so loud, I would probably have never told her anything.

# Chapter 21
# Please Take Me Home

INSTEAD OF TAKING the bus back to *the place*, I called Dr. Ramsey for a ride from Janie's house. I wanted to only be in the presence of those I trusted.

"Dr. Ramsey, can you pick me up and take me to the shelter tonight?"

"Boy, you must think I'm stupid," Dr. Ramsey chuckled, throwing me off. "I am not your chauffer, nor your guardian angel. I'm busy."

"But Doc, I need you. I'm at my girlfriend's house, and I just told her about the thing."

"Are you OK?"

"Yes and no, Doc. Physically, I'm fine, but mentally … I could really use a lifeline right now."

"I'm on my way. Text me the address, Mr. Salimu."

When he arrived, I felt like a giant weight had been lifted off my chest. I still had a huge lump in my throat, but his support made me stronger.

The drive from Janie's house to the shelter would take more than two hours, and I knew it was plenty of time for a thorough mentorship session.

"So, Mr. Salimu, who is this Janie girl I have heard so little about?"

"Sir, I've told you about her before. Same lady that taught me how to do a backflip and likes to laugh a lot. She taught me how to play piano too."

"Mr. Salimu, what you just said is the extent of my knowledge about this person. Why have I not seen her around Crenshaw High?"

"Doc, she does not go to Crenshaw."

"Since you are being so cryptic, why don't you at least explain to me why I'm out here driving your ass around!"

I explained to Dr. Ramsey how I confessed everything to Janie and how she reacted. I asked Doc whether crying myself to sleep in front of my girlfriend made me less of a man.

The whole drive then became one very long conversation about manhood, character, and responsibility. Doc told me what real masculinity was. He told me that I needed to forget about what I learned from movies and TV shows. He flipped my concerns upside-down and showed me that I was not weak. I had a feeling that he would have such a perspective, but hearing him preach it to me really lifted my spirit.

"Yohancé, being more in touch with your feelings does not make you less of a man," Dr. Ramsey said. I could tell that he wanted to say so much more, but he had always kept our conversations very professional. Tonight I felt like something different was about to happen.

"Yohancé, you may not know this about me, but I am a gay man, and that does not make me any less of a man."

There was a long pause as Dr. Ramsey moved his gaze from the road to eye the disbelief on his passenger's face.

"What I am trying to say here, Mr. Salimu, is that your sexual preferences, level of promiscuity, emotions, and desires are not what makes you a man. Whether someone is more effeminate or *macho* does not make them more or less of a man, either. Being a man is all about responsibility, commitment, and generally taking care of shit. *How* you take care of shit determines what kind of a man you are. When you were vulnerable and told Janie about what happened to you, you showed how much of a man you truly are. You didn't hide from your problems or sweep them under the rug; you faced them and shared your regrets. Tears do not make you less of a man, Yohancé! They make you a different kind of man; A more complete man."

"I hear you, Doc, I do … I just …"

"What is it, Mr. Salimu? Are you still not clear about what it means to be a man?"

"No, it's not that, Doc. I just thought I was really good at figuring out when someone was gay, and yet, here you've been all along."

"I'm sorry to have to tell you this, Yohancé, but your perception of people is not perfect. If it were, then you and I would probably not be having this conversation right now."

"Touché, Dr. Ramsey! Touché! I needed that one, Doc."

"That was a lot of energy I just used telling you all that. I need some food. Mr. Salimu, what are we eating?"

"Let's go to the best restaurant in LA, Doc. Taco Bell. We can have the dinner of champions."

Dr. Ramsey chuckled as we pulled into the drive-thru lane. He thought my obsession with fast food was unhealthy, but he would indulge me that day.

"You have to slow down, Yohancé, the food is not going anywhere," Dr. Ramsey exclaimed as I finished half my meal before we left the drive-thru.

"Doc, it's unnatural to eat food slowly when it tastes this good," I said through a mouthful of nachos.

Dr. Ramsey was disgusted and insisted that I slow down before I choked. I did as he asked, because I was so grateful that he bought me dinner. I thanked him and apologized for my behavior, which kick-started the rest of our conversation. We conversed about character and responsibility in great detail, until the traffic started to build. Doc needed to focus more on driving. There was a sudden loud screech, and a jolt. My Taco Bell meal flew out of my lap and exploded upon contact with the dashboard. Dr. Ramsey was screaming at a car that had just cut us off. There were beans and rice everywhere. He offered to buy me a replacement meal, but I told him I had had my fill.

This was one of the biggest lies I had ever told in my entire life, because I was always hungry. For years, I had to fight for every meal I received. And losing my meal in that near-accident pushed me over the edge. The Universe was trying to tell me that not only did I have to fight for everything I got, but when I received my prize, there was no guarantee I could keep it. There was always a fight.

Two hours of driving proved to not be long enough to discuss everything, so when we arrived at the shelter, we parked in order to wrap up our conversation.

"We should talk about your plans for the summer break, Mr. Salimu."

"I'm taking a few classes at your alma mater, UCLA. Then I might land a job at the Aerospace Corporation. Finally, I will be going to football practice when it starts. What more is there to say?"

Dr. Ramsey warned me that I would have competition from others who also thought they were the smartest kids at their high school.

"Yeah, yeah, Doc. I get it. Big fish, little fish. Little pond, big pond. I've heard it all before, but I'm still better than all of them."

"You might want to exercise some humility, Mr. Salimu."

"Doc, this faux overconfidence is the only reason I'm still standing. When I say I got this, or everything is going to be OK, I'm not just trying to convince you ... I need to hear it too."

"Yohancé, are you still confident that the Aerospace Corporation is going to offer you the job?"

"Yes, sir. I've been praying on it too, and my prayers typically get answered one way or another."

"I didn't know you were religious, Yohancé."

"Yeah, that's because my ego has always been louder than my faith. Some things I just keep to myself."

"Have you been keeping the secret to yourself of why you think you need to play football, Mr. Salimu?"

"Doc, you lost me. What do you mean by that?"

"What I'm getting at, Mr. Salimu, is, why are you going to play this brutal sport that could get you hurt, when you are so very gifted academically?"

"Dr. Ramsey, the reason I want to play football is because I'm smart enough to understand my true nature, and brave enough to not run from it. Sometimes a teenage boy just wants to sprint really fast, break people, and hurt things—and that's OK. People spend so much time demonizing the phrase 'boys will be boys,' but there is some real truth to that. In the safest and most disciplined way I can, I'm going to let out some of this aggression in my heart. I know you are not a fan of the sport, but one day you might come to terms with how deep and vital of a purpose football serves in our society."

"OK, Mr. Salimu. Whenever you are ready to get off your soapbox, you can exit my car," Dr. Ramsey said sarcastically. "Just do me a favor: make sure that you're not the one getting hurt."

# Half-Time

"I realized that I can't do this all on my own. I'm no Superman."

*I had to lick my wounds and get back out there!*

# Not A Chapter:
# A Time for Reflection

THERE IS NOTHING more humbling to a man than being raped. The fact that someone had their way with my body has profoundly shaped me as a human being. I would not say the experience has made me a humble person, though. It has simply kept me grounded and prevented my ego from transcending into arrogance.

**CONTINUATION SHEET**

Los Angeles Police Department

| PAGE NO. 3/10 | TYPE OF REPORT | Crime and Arrest | | | BOOKING NO. Non-releasable | OR NO. 13659 0906 |
|---|---|---|---|---|---|---|
| ITEM NO. | OU AN | ARTICLE | SERIAL NO | BRAND | MODEL NO. | MISC DESCRIPTION (EG. COLOR, SIZE, INSCRIPTIONS, CALIBER, REVOLVER, ETC) | DOLLAR VALUE |

**SOURCE OF ACTIVITY:**
On May 6, 2009 at approximately 2330 hrs, my partner Officer Branley #37120 and I Officer Faulkner #39546 were assigned to Hollywood Division patrol 6A79. We were in full uniform driving a marked black and white police vehicle. When we received a radio call "Station Call" Inc # 090506006084 RD636

**INVESTIGATION:**
On May 6, 2009 at approximately 2350 hours my partner and I responded to Hollywood police station to conduct a follow up for a possible rape suspect. At the station we were met by Officer Escobar # 38230 and Officer Nunez #36181 working 16X82 in Foothill division. They advised us the Victim (Yohance S.) had been raped and claimed to know where the suspect lives. We conducted a follow up investigation at 6364 Yucca Room# 106 to see if the possible suspect was still at the location. Once at the location we knocked on the door and identified ourselves several times. We could hear movement inside of the hotel room, but the occupant refused to open the door. We obtained the pin code from the manger to open the door. We entered the hotel room and detained the suspect without incident. We conducted a field show up at scene at which time the Victim positively identified the suspect. Unit 6A65 Officer Camacho #38554 and Officer Perez #34887 transported the suspect to Santa Monica UCLA Hospital the Rape and Treatment center. My partner and I transported the victim to the same location approximately 15 minutes later.

While at UCLA I interviewed the victim. He stated that on May 6, 2009 at approximately 1900 hours, he was walking to the train station located on Vine and Hollywood, when a female later identified as suspect ( Rachel ) who is a male approached him and stated, "You have a nice butt." The victim replied, "Thanks." The suspect asked the victim if he would like to go back to his place. The victim asked the suspect, "Why, what are we doing to do?" The suspect replied, "We're going to fuck." The victim replied, "No, I'm only 15 years old." The suspect asked the victim if he had a curfew. The victim replied , "No." The suspect grabbed the victim by his right wrist and stated, "It will only be a few minutes." The victim went with the suspect to his hotel room and started to watch T.V. Moments later the suspect removed the victim pants and told the victim, "Turn over and lay on your belly." The victim stated, "No, you take off your clothes now." The suspect replied, "No not yet, I like it like this and I want to massage your butt." The victim turned over and the suspect poured lotion on his butt and began to massage it. The victim thought it seemed kind of weird so he turned back around and said, "Take off your clothes now!" The suspect replied, " Ok, but I want to do it my way first. Then you can do what you want with me." Then oral copulated the victim. The victim turned over again after the suspect took his shirt off. A few minutes later the victim felt an unknown object penetrate his anus. The victim jumped up, quickly turned around and asked the suspect, "What the fuck was that?" The Suspect replied, "It was my finger." The victim said, "What's up with you? Are you a transsexual?" The suspect replied, "No, I'm a female." The suspect told the victim to turn back around and not to look back. The victim did as the suspect said, felt the suspect mount him and felt something penetrate his anus for a second time. The victim then quickly turned around again and said, "Man, what is that? Are you sure you don't have a dick?" The suspect replied, "No, I don't. It just my finger." The victim made several attempts to feel if the suspect had a penis but the suspect would move away and slap his hand. The victim said, "Fuck this, I'm leaving, you're fucking weird!". The victim put his clothes back

My rape through the eyes of LAPD

**CONTINUATION SHEET**

Los Angeles Police Department

| PAGE NO. 3 1/0 | TYPE OF REPORT | | Crime and Arrest | | | BOOKING NO. Non-releasable | DR NO. 13\_\_\_\_ 0906 |

| ITEM NO. | QU AN | ARTICLE | SERIAL NO | BRAND | MODEL NO. | MISC DESCRIPTION (EG. COLOR, SIZE, INSCRIPTIONS, CALIBER, REVOLVER, ETC) | DOLLAR VALUE |
|---|---|---|---|---|---|---|---|

on and left the room. As the victim proceed to walk down the corridor of the hotel, he grabbed his butt because it felt weird. The suspect yelled to the victim, "Yeah, that was a dick in you." The victim went to his residence and spoke with a friend who told the victim to call police because he had just been raped.

**ARREST:**

Non-releasable

**BOOKING:**

Non-releasable

**INJURIES / MEDICAL TREATEMENT:**
The Victim and the suspect were treated at the Santa Monica – UCLA Medical Center – Rape Treatment Center by Dr. Lawson, Kisha

**PHOTOGRAPHS:**
None

**EVIDENCE:**
All evidence was booked at PAB property. See attached property report.

**ADDITIONAL:**
None

**COURT INFORMATION:**
My partner and I can testify to the information contained in this report.

Police report from LAPD

The police report is not included for shock value, proof, or validation. It is there because it is the biggest failure of the first half that I need to reflect on. When a football coach is in the locker room after the first half of a game, this is how upfront they are about the team's shortcomings. They put it all out there so that the team can see their mistakes and make adjustments for the next half.

I failed to protect myself. I allowed my promiscuity, my ego, and my *lust* to take charge of my life. In my favorite poem ("If," by Rudyard Kipling), there is a part that goes,

If you can force your heart and nerve and sinew

To serve your turn long after they are gone,

And so hold on when there is nothing in you

Except the Will which says to them: 'Hold on!'

I felt gone, so how was I going to hold on now? Where was I going to find the "Will" to keep going?

Do you know where I found that "Will"? It was in that voice in my head all along—my ego. I started reflecting on where I'd been, and how I was not really *a product of my environment*. Sure, there were a couple of times when I dodged a few bullets here and there, but overall I was intact. I was *me*. I could be in the middle of a race war and I was still confident that I could sneak my way into the lunchroom. I could do a few stretches and miraculously be handed a jersey like I was a member of the best football team in the city. I could enter a knife fight with just a blanket and come out unscathed. I could talk with senior-level engineers at the Aerospace Corporation and convince them to interview me for a job that was far above my expertise.

That inner voice in my head made me think I could do anything. After my reflection I realized that I was the shit! I realized that nothing was going to stand in my way as I drove toward success, not even being *raped* by the most beautiful transgender person in Hollywood!

# Section 3 / Third Quarter

Ready to prove myself

*I'm ready for whatever, Coach! Put me in the game!*

# Chapter 22
# Summer Grind: Competing at UCLA

MAKING MY WAY through Westwood to attend my first class on the campus of UCLA felt intimidating. The whole college town was located right outside the campus. It was vibrant and easy to get lost in. I assumed two things about everyone I walked past in that little town. One: they were enrolled at UCLA, and two: they must be smarter than me. "Excuse me, do you know where Boelter Hall is?" I queried this cute Asian girl who was covered head to toe in UCLA gear.

"Boelter Hall? You must be a freshman," the girl said, then gave directions to my first class. I knew that taking classes at UCLA for the summer was going to be awesome, just by how big this girl's smile was. There was some shock and awe in her eyes as she gazed up at me. She probably thought I was some big-time recruit even though I had yet to start my junior year of high school. I wasn't going to ruin her fantasy.

The classroom at UCLA felt a lot different from the ones at Crenshaw High. The biggest difference for me was in my outlook. I did not instantly feel like I was the smartest student in the room. I was no longer competing against Rodney and Kolmus. It was time to find a new group to compete against. But who in this classroom was the smartest?

The first exam in my college statistics class was given to all students attending the program. A bell curve graph explained how each one of us was faring in the course. This was enough for me to know who I needed to compete against. I was number five on the board out of thirty students. Being in the top five was not bad, but I had to figure out who were the four individuals scoring higher than me. The program was a mixture of rising juniors and seniors, and only one representative of any high school was present. I was competing against the best of Beverly Hills High School, Diamond Bar High School, Palos Verdes High School, and many more top-ranking schools in the city of Los Angeles. But if they thought that Crenshaw High was going to be on the bottom of that bell curve, they had another thing coming. Crenshaw was the best athletically; we had been slaughtering these other schools in every sport for decades. But that wasn't enough; now I was going to show them that we handled our business in the classroom, as well.

The fierce intensity of this competition was mostly in my head, though. These were some of the nicest and happiest kids I had ever met. When we headed to lunch break, most of the kids would sit together and study over a meal. Fearing they might get the upper hand over me, I never turned down an invitation to a study session. The program gave us a stipend to buy food on the campus, which was how I was able to blend in at the study sessions. Most of the other students supplemented their meals with their pocket money because the daily stipend was so small. All I needed to do was buy something small with the stipend so I could participate in all the sessions. I'd usually get a burrito or muffin to nibble on as I took notes on all the good information being shared. I wasn't going to let being poor be an excuse for not climbing up to the number one spot.

Most of my peers in the program acted very differently than my peers back at Crenshaw, and it took me some time to find out why. This student population, unlike at Crenshaw, was not all black or Hispanic kids. When I took a step back to observe us, we almost resembled the rainbow with how very different we were as a group. Culturally, spiritually, socio-economically, and racially, we were all incredibly different from one another. The kid with Indian heritage was the first one to realize this, as he joked that we were not the best our school could offer. Rather, we were the best of whatever color of the rainbow the program was trying to fill a slot with. But we grew closer through learning about one another's differences.

As we progressed through our statistics and robotics courses, I became more spiteful toward the kid who was in the number-one spot. His name was James, and he made me feel angry or insecure. He never ate with the rest of us or shared in discussions outside of class. It's not because he was the quiet type; he frequently smirked and shot quick remarks to correct other students.

James was a tall white guy with bright, shiny blond hair, broad shoulders, and piercing blue eyes that felt menacing as he gazed at me. I had never met anyone who looked quite like him, and I wondered why I felt such deep negative feelings toward him. Was he a deeply racist person that wanted me, the black boy from the hood, to look stupid in class? Was he committed to making me fail? None of his actions justified these accusations, but something about him gave off a horrible aura.

I continued to feel animosity toward James—until the day I finally beat him at something. Our instructor had invited the whole class to stay late. During this time, the instructor wanted to test us by administering riddles and mathematical philosophies we had to solve. Most of the students in the bottom half of the class left within the first hour. The top five were hanging tight. We all wanted to prove we were smarter than one another, so we sat in that room for hours, trying to solve every puzzle our instructor threw at us. James had solved most problems on his own, while the rest of us worked as a team. At one point, James had solved six problems. The rest of us, five. His excessive ego was very familiar to me, but watching someone else flourish in this trait made me hate how deeply rooted in my own character this flaw was.

By sheer luck, my team managed to tie with James. Thus, the instructor declared the next problem to be the final tiebreaker. The instructor drew a mixture of symbols and numbers on the board using several different color markers. It stretched the entire length of the room. Instead of joining my team to discuss the problem, I walked right up to the board. The message just unfolded for me. I turned to the instructor.

"Sir, I think I got it," I said in triumph. "The answer is: Too wise you are. Too wise you be. Too wise you are. Too wise for me."

The instructor began to clap, as my team exploded into cheers. He informed us that the original anagram was not his, but that he'd added multiple layers of complexity to it and never expected anyone to solve it.

As everyone packed their bags to leave, James tapped me on the shoulder.

"Yohancé, you're really very smart. I learned something from you today."

"Oh yeah, James? What's that?"

"Just that sometimes it's better to work as a team. Sometimes."

"Thanks James … Umm … Can I ask you something?"

"Yeah, what's up, dude?" he said with a smile that I could not trust as he gazed at me with those piercing blue eyes.

"Why do I feel so much fear when you look at me? I get this really negative feeling around you." I was not afraid to hear his response. If he hated me, I was ready to hear it. If, because of the color of my skin, he despised how close our intellect was, I wanted to know. It was time for him to stop being nice or faking like we could ever be friends.

"Yohancé, I'm sorry you feel that way, but you're not the first person to say something like this to me. Come closer; I want to show you something."

James's request scared me, but I knew I had to do it. I was not going to be afraid of this guy for some unknown or prejudiced reason. I could never have expected what he told me. James had a fake left eye. That is, it was made of glass. He lost the eye to cancer as a kid. The diagnosis was discovered after James took a photo as a child. He explained that people usually have a red glow out of their eyes when a picture is taken with flash. But his eye glowed white, a sure sign that he had this type of ocular cancer.

I was not really looking for racism, but when I found out it wasn't there, a wave of relief washed over me. My anxious feelings were now replaced by embarrassment. I had waited to nearly the end of the program to find out that James was actually an OK guy who just didn't have free time to study with the rest of us. He was busy helping run his family's business. We did get to hang out though, as our instructor paraded us around the university, trying to convince us that there was no better school for us than UCLA. James seemed sold, but I knew I was headed to the United States Air Force Academy.

I learned a lesson from James. No matter where I go, there will be someone like James to compete with. I thought I had been through a lot in life at that point, but comparing myself to James made me feel weak. He had already wrestled with cancer, and he won. Finding out something like that based on a flash from a camera made his story even crazier. I remember feeling a bit jealous and wishing I could take a big flash photo so I could check that I did not have some rare cancer in my eye.

The next day, which was supposed to be the last day of the program, I got my wish. They say be careful what you wish for, but my desire was only a small thought, not a wish, a hope, or a prayer. I was walking to my classroom in Royce Hall, and there was a film crew in an adjacent hallway prepping their equipment. One of the cameramen must have been strobing their flash periodically in this empty hallway. When I walked past the men, I caught a full blast of bright light that disoriented me. I walked out of the building to collect myself, but I could not see well. The edges of my vision were turning black and closing into a small circle that had limited focus. My head was throbbing with pain as I set my bookbags down. Suddenly I collapsed onto the ground. People told me they were calling an ambulance and to keep breathing. But I could not see their faces.

I heard the ambulance drive up, and an EMT guy asked my name.

Still a wiseass, even in a health crisis, I was going to do this fancy and artistic way of telling him my name. But I could not remember how to do it. I couldn't even remember my own name.

"Dude, I have no idea what my name is right now, and I am freaking out about it. My head hurts a lot, and I can't really see anything."

"That's OK. Do I have permission to go through your pockets?"

He was confused because he found a Crenshaw I.D. when he thought I was a UCLA student.

"Are you a student here, Mr. Salimu?" the EMT asked.

I touched my bookbag and rationalized that I must be a student, so I said, "Yeah, I think so. UCLA ... I'm a Bruin, right?"

"According to this I.D. you go to Crenshaw High School, Mr. Salimu."

"I'm not trying to lie to you sir, I just don't know the answer to these questions. Can we get out of the sun? My head is throbbing, and I think I'm about to vomit."

A man with this deep, booming, monotone voice—he sounded black—burst through the crowd and started answering all the EMT's questions. The next thing I knew, he was riding with me in the back of an ambulance. This man explained that he was one of my instructors at UCLA—which meant I was a Bruin, right?

When we arrived at the hospital, I could see again and I was already feeling like my usual smartass self. So why were all the questions going to the big guy instead of me?

"We heard you screaming," one of the doctors said. "What is your pain level, Mr. Salimu?"

"Ten out of ten, and I don't think I was screaming."

"I will be back shortly, but the nurse standing right next to you isn't going anywhere."

A nurse suddenly appeared. Someone put something in my arm, and the lights all went off.

There was a familiar face sitting next to me when I woke up. I was in a lot less pain, so I figured I could joke around with this medical doctor.

"Waddup, Dr. Ramsey."

"How are you feeling Mr. Salimu?"

"Like a million bucks Doc. We should be able to get out of here soon."

"Mr. Salimu, why am I your emergency contact for this summer program?"

"Because you are the only one who answers my call when I need you, Doc."

"As heartwarming as that is, Yohancé, you could have given them your mother's phone number."

"Doc, what if she doesn't pay her cell phone bill the month I need her? What if she just isn't available? You being here right now is proof that I made the right choice."

"I spoke with your instructor out there, but he would not tell me how you fared in the courses."

"Doc, it went just like I told you it would. I kicked some butt."

"Did the other students prove to you how much harder you have to work to compete with them?"

"I was not the best, Doc, but still one of the best. And that's good enough for me."

"It sounds like you were slacking, Mr. Salimu. Are you planning to take that same attitude with you to the Aerospace Corporation?"

"How did you know I got the job, Doc?"

"You told me when *you* pray for things, they usually happen, and I never doubted you."

"Yeah, but sometimes I just say stuff like that to convince myself that it's true. My new boss called me only two days ago and told me I could start working whenever I was ready."

"And are you ready?" Dr. Ramsey queried as he looked me up and down in my hospital bed.

"Doc, I was born ready. I could use your help with something, though."

"Yohancé, you must truly think I have wings on my back and infinite patience for your buffoonery. What is it that the great King Yohancé requests of me, such a feeble peasant?"

As Dr. Ramsey bowed to me, I laughed very hard at his joke. I felt almost 100 percent better, thanks to his sense of humor.

"Dr. Ramsey, can I borrow some slacks and a dress shirt for work? I want to convince the people at the Aerospace Corporation that I fit in."

"Now the master wants my clothes!? He shall have them, he shall! What more can I give to thee, oh great King Yohancé?"

I was howling by now at Dr. Ramsey's performance.

"Sir, I could also use some dress shoes, but I don't think we wear the same size. I can bum those from someone else."

"If it pleases the crown, I shall also supply a pair of cheap dress shoes. You better pay me back, though. You are nobody's charity case, you hear me?"

I chuckled and agreed. He knew all too well how much I hated taking charity.

But there wasn't enough money in the world to pay back Dr. Ramsey for all he had done for me. He really was my guardian angel.

# Chapter 23
## Too Good to Be a Gangsta?

NO ONE ELSE wanted out as bad as Kumasi and I. The kids at the shelter seemed content with their lives and happy to act like everything was normal. We were not normal. We were all at the bottom. We were all losers simply by our circumstances. We were all at that rock bottom starting place, and everyone else seemed happy even if they were to lose this race. Not us.

I wanted to tell Kumasi that he could not hang out with the other kids in the shelter, but I was not his father. I could not tell Kumasi with any real authority whom he could and could not befriend.

The kids scheming and playing games in the rec room were all Kumasi had. He did not have mountains of schoolwork to keep him busy, or a boatload of programs to focus his attention. Convincing Kumasi that there were better things to do than hang out with kids at the shelter was futile.

I slipped out when the shelter programs were held. My go-to was always the same—basketball. I found a public outdoor basketball court by the train station, and even though I didn't know anyone in the neighborhood, I knew I could get selected to play in a few streetball pick-up games. If I was a few years younger, I might have been afraid to play basketball with so many strangers covered in tattoos. Being from the hood has a strange effect on people, though. Every time I walked into a new "dangerous neighborhood," I always found myself comparing it to where I came from. There was no such thing as danger anymore, because I already survived the Jungles. Everything else was child's play. None of these new gangbangers scared me, and none of their shady deals on the side of the basketball courts surprised me. I wasn't acting tough; I was tough, and I just wanted to play some ball.

I don't usually do a lot of smack talk when I am playing sports. That doesn't mean I am humble, though. I'm usually grinning and laughing at my opponents. Inside, I'm coming up with funny jokes for my own amusement. When my hubris does show, it usually pisses my opponents off, and they get more violent. It's just part of my competitive nature. If I am mismatched in a basketball game, I typically warn the guy guarding me to protect himself.

Mismatches happen quite often too. It was the summer of 2009, and the team captains at this park had never seen me ball. They picked me to be on a team, but the bum on the opposing team guarding me was certainly not my equal.

"Don't tell me what to do! I know how to play basketball, young blood!"

I had no idea why my team wanted me to guard this old bum. The only reason he looked close to my size was all the extra clothing he was wearing, and he stunk so bad that I did not want to touch him. The whole game, I was roughing this guy up and laughing at how frustrated he was getting. I don't play by the same rules as those prima donnas who get paid millions of dollars to prance around a fancy gymnasium. This forty-year-old bum was not going to catch a break from me; I came to play.

Pretty soon, everyone at the courts—plus the gangbangers on the sidelines—noticed how much of a savage I was being to this old homeless dude. My team was already winning, but I would not be satisfied until I embarrassed this bum for all the smack he was talking. In retrospect, I think everyone at the park thought I was bullying this guy because he was a bum. On the contrary, I saw him as my equal—at least socioeconomically. We were both homeless. He just looked the part better than I did. I saw him as my possible future, which was the only reason I hit him so hard when he lashed out at me.

I always have this really twisted smile on my face when I am in a fight. It's because I am having fun. When I finished throwing my short combo, all I could think about was how I was just another bum in a bum fight. I wasn't only whooping this bum's ass now, I was laughing hysterically as I did it. He lunged at me, and I punched him right in his nose. I was ready for the fight to continue, but a couple of ladies came out of nowhere and started scolding me for disrespecting my elders. They "broke up" the fight and continued to berate me until a small group of gang members told them to shut the fuck up and get away from their new homie. They were talking about me. Man, that felt good.

What they saw was a ruthless teenager beat up an old man and laugh at him for stinking up the basketball court in more ways than one. They did not see the irony: I was fighting to distance myself from a future that I was now falling into.

"Nigga, you gave that bum the hands! Whats yo name, blood?"

I thought about not introducing myself and just walking away, but these guys seemed so thrilled to meet me. I wanted to see if I could actually get invited into their gang, so I treated the whole exchange like an interview. I told them my name and that I lived a long ways away from the park, and that I was fixin' to catch a bus back home. They told me that I wasn't catchin' no busses. I could catch a ride home with the homies.

The leader of the gang wanted to introduce me to everyone before we left the park. We walked around for a bit shaking hands with people posted up all around the park. I never knew how much influence he had on the whole place until he showed me how extensive his operation was. He wasn't just some thug ... he was smart. I felt like I had to show him that I was smart too. We talked about math, science, charisma, determination, discipline, and a myriad of topics that I never thought could flourish in the mind of a gang member. If the bum I had just beat up was living one of my possible futures, surely I was staring at another one as I spoke with this gang leader. He had women, he had money, he had power, and he wanted to show it all to me.

As we pulled up in front of the shelter, still talking, I was doing some figuring. Yeah, I was homeless, but I was smart enough to take this gang leader's place, and do better for myself and my family. I could be him. I could be better than him, but still him. I told him that I had just finished a summer program at UCLA and that they had given us business cards. I handed the gang leader my business card as I got out of the car. He looked at it, cursed, and tore it up.

"Yohancé, you can't join our gang. You deserve to find another way to succeed, like school or some shit. Go get that life. Be something. And re-member me, 'cause I'm saving yo ass for real by saying no to you. Peace."

I never saw my new homies ever again.

# Chapter 24
## Don't Pity the Fool

IT WAS FOOLISH of me to think I had already reached my finish line. Of course I couldn't become another gangster or statistic in South-Central Los Angeles. I had plans. I was planning on becoming the captain of a bunch of sports teams and school clubs, and a top student academically. For the most part, I knew exactly how I was going to make it happen, too.

Me: Running faster than the football players and talking shit

I've always been a strategic planner, but when it came to the specifics of rejoining the football team, I had truly dropped the ball. There was no way I could *sneak* my way onto the team again. And I'd been talking shit all spring during Track and Field practice, telling the football players I was coming for their spot. I was getting bigger, faster, and stronger. And I'd told everyone what my next move would be, except for the one man who mattered the most: G-Man.

Summer football practice was starting soon, around the same time as my new job. And I had a decision to make. Was I going to forget about football or make a last-minute effort to rejoin the team? I decided to phone a friend first.

"Kolmus, I'm about to go up to the Shaw and ask G-Man if I can rejoin the team."

"Aight then, Yohancé. It was nice knowin' you," Kolmus said solemnly.

"Whatta you mean? G-Man can be an understanding guy," I said back.

"If you think he gone *understand* you, and ain't gone kill yo black ass, then why you callin' me?"

"Because I need my best friend's help figuring some shit out, that's why," I said as my patience shrank.

"OK. OK," Kolmus said, as if preparing to tell another joke. "So, how you gon' get that nigga G-Man to let you on the team, bro?"

"Kolmus, what the fuck do you think I called you for? If a nigga could figure this shit out on his own, then I wouldn't be calling yo bitch ass." (Only best friends can talk to each other like this.)

Kolmus was a little more serious when he replied, "Yeah, bro, I hear you, but I mean … I don't even go to that school no more, so maybe I'm not the best person to ask."

"Naa, Kolmus. You definitely the best dude to ask."

"OK, let me think," Kolmus said as he took a long pause. "Yohancé, you remember when we was in second grade and we all got sent to the principal's office for playing that game on the playground?"

"You mean 'Slap That Healthy Butt'?" I replied in disbelief that he remembered that game.

"Exactly! We was all running around at recess playing a school-wide game of grab ass, boys vs. girls. Shit was wild," Kolmus exclaimed, laughing throughout his explanation.

"I remember that. For some reason I think everyone in our grade year got sent home that day, except me," I said, pondering this little mystery.

"Exactly, bro. It's because you started crying when the principal walked in. You sold that shit!"

"So, let me get this straight. You want me to start fake crying in front of G-Man like a lil bitch?"

Kolmus's tone got a bit defensive when he replied, "Yohancé, I'm not sayin' to be fake. I don't know, bro, it's up to you what you wanna do."

"I'm thinking I'll just tell G-Man the truth. I'll tell him why I didn't play football my sophomore year," I said feigning confidence.

"Yohancé, you gone tell him *everything*? Like about being homeless and shit?" Kolmus knew many of my secrets, but I'd never tell him about Rachel. In that moment, I thought maybe I would have to tell G-Man about her. I was scared.

"Kolmus, I'm going to tell him whatever he needs to hear. I just hope he doesn't pity me. I ain't tryna be nobody's charity case."

"You might need him to pity you just a little bit. Yohancé, this could work."

"You think so?"

"Yeah … Good luck, ma nigga. Fingers crossed G-Man doesn't slap the shit out yo bitch ass."

One by one we knocked on G-Man's door to *interview* for a spot on his football team. Everybody wanted to be a Crenshaw Cougar. And everybody and they momma wanted to be on the football team. When it was finally my turn, I walked into the office with my head high and my chest stuck out. The blue and gold tiled flooring extended toward a giant desk that was covered in trophies. Behind the desk sat G-Man, with his aviator sunglasses, wild hair shooting out the sides of his ball cap, and clenched fists lying heavy on a stack of papers.

Standing outside of G-Man's office, July 2009

"Well, good afternoon to you, YOH-HON-SAY! What can I do for you, sir?"

"Umm, G-Man, I um … I want to join the football team."

"No, you don't! You quit on us already, YOH-HON-SAY. This football team ain't too important to you, so why don't you just walk on out my office and send the next guy in here."

G-Man's words hurt, but I didn't argue, because I couldn't find my voice. All the confidence I walked into the room with had evaporated away as a giant lump settled in my throat. But I was frozen in my shoes. Unable to walk away, I stood still as my punishment continued.

"This Crenshaw football team is too much of a commitment for you, YOH-HON-SAY. Isn't that why you said you quit last time? What's changed, huh? You just gone quit on us again anyhow."

I made my mind up to open my mouth and say something profound, but as soon as I spoke, my voice cracked.

"G-Man, I'm homeless, and I need something to commit myself to," I said as warm tears escaped my eyes. "At first I thought I couldn't handle it, and that's why I left. I'm staying in a shelter about two hours from here with my mom and little brother, but I promise you I can make every practice. I want to be on this team and …"

Before I could embarrass myself any further, G-Man stopped me and asked, "How are you eating? Are you getting enough food?"

"I'm mostly only eating here at school. I really miss the extra food I used to get when I was on the football team. But I'm making it work. I basically live out of my locker here at school."

"Come here, Yohancé," G-Man said as he stood up from his chair. I started walking around G-Man's desk, not knowing what to expect. Whatever happened next was going to be my fault. G-Man didn't want a bunch of whiny little bitches on his team, and I was showing just how much of a sissy I was.

When I finished my one-hundred-mile walk around G-Man's desk, I saw him raise his hand in a motion all too familiar. G-Man's hand came down with a swipe as he grabbed his keys off the desk and kindly asked me to follow him. He didn't hit me. But where was he taking me?

G-Man walked me deep into the football locker room into a part I'd never seen before. Who knew there was a dark, hidden section of the locker room at the Shaw? Once there, he handed me eight strips of paper.

"Everyone else gets two, but I'm giving you a few extra lockers back here as well. Equipment issue is tomorrow as soon as summer school is done for the day."

"Thanks, G-Man," I said as I wiped my face. "I'll leave my job early and make sure I get here on time."

"Job? Yohancé, I don't let my players hold a summer job while they are in football camp."

"G-Man, I really need the money, and I know I can do both at the same time."

"I don't think it's going to work out, YOH-HON-SAY, but you have my blessing to try. And if it doesn't work out, you will still have access to these lockers. I ain't takin' nothin' away from ya."

# Chapter 25
# Summer Grind: Work and Football Practice

IT WAS FINALLY happening. After running through a fire storm of red tape, I had my first job. I had travelled halfway across the city to get my health and drug test completed. That hospital was much fancier than any place I had ever been. The documents for my background check and security clearance wanted to know the names of almost everyone I had ever known in my life. I spent most of my time on the phone as I filled them out. I had to call everyone and ask if it was OK if I gave their name, telephone number, and address to the government as a reference. The section where they asked for information on every sibling I had proved to be the most difficult. That was the day I found out that I do not have sixteen siblings—there are actually eighteen of us.

It can get difficult to count the rungs of a ladder when you have never seen the top. After all this information was processed and I received my security badge, I was ready to start my first day of work.

"Welcome to the Aerospace Corporation," said our presenter as we sat down at the large, rectangular table in the center of the room. The room was dark and metallic, with a dark silver glow emanating from the floor and walls. We were given an impressive overview of the company, which made me feel out of place. I was wearing a bright peach-colored dress shirt, khakis, a brown belt, and brown dress shoes. My hair was very short, and I had a full, trimmed goatee. I was trying to look as mature and professional as possible. All was going smoothly—until the presenter asked us a question.

"Who is the youngest person joining our company today?" he said. He only asked, he explained, because the Aerospace Corporation's median age was quite high, with so many mature engineers refusing to retire from such a great company.

One of the ladies at the table proudly raised her hand and, after looking around the room, suggested it must be her. She was twenty-seven, and this was only her second job after Raytheon. Before I could stop myself, my hand shot up and I had already spoken.

"Yeah, but I'm only sixteen, so I win."

Everyone in the room stared at me. Not only for my juvenile outburst, but because they didn't believe me. I made a note to myself that I needed to start acting older than my age if I was going to work here.

After the orientation briefing, I left the giant corporate building to cross the campus and meet my new team in laboratory 6. I was going to be a lab technician for a defense contractor for the United States Air Force. My job was to build and evaluate space batteries and flight cells for the energy systems on our nation's satellites. And somehow the skills I had learned from my F.I.R.S.T. Robotics Team #1692 made me qualified to do all of this. I didn't have to lie to myself and say that I was ready, because I had a yellow cartoon sponge in my head already taking care of it. Over and over, in my head, I continued to try to convince myself that I was ready as I swiped my security badge to enter the facility.

**Work**

The laboratory was cold. I walked in and was greeted by a familiar face.

"Good morning, good morning, good morning, Yohancé. Glad to finally have you here!" said Alonzo.

"Good morning, sir," I said with a big smile.

"Yohancé, its Alonzo, not sir. We are on a first-name basis here."

Alonzo introduced me to the whole team that day: Simon, Sarah, Jim, Sharon, Chiboisee, Jason, Jasen, and Ryan. I would mostly work with Jasen and Jason. Alonzo made sure all was cool and then left, saying he would come back to check on me later in the day. Jasen and Jason were very hospitable people; they helped me set up my desk workstation and my lab workstation so I could start proving my worth.

Jasen pointed to a corner of the lab where I saw several big metal boxes with wires sticking out of them. I thought that he was going to have me do some plebe housecleaning. Not quite.

"Yohancé, I need you to reverse engineer, multiply, and make blueprints for that device. Currently only Jason knows how to make them, because he designed them."

"Wow! I actually know how to do that, guys!" I said with a huge amount of relief in my voice.

Jason shot back, "Dude, it wouldn't matter if you didn't. Alonzo said you're smart as heck. Anything you don't know how to do, we'll teach you."

"Hey, Jason, since you designed the box and most of my questions will go toward you for now, is it OK if I call you Asian Jason? Just to avoid confusion."

"Dude, I think that's hilarious. Yeah, call me Asian Jason, so you don't confuse white Jasen over there."

Jasen cracked a huge smile and laughed, "Hey, I never gave you permission to call me white Jasen."

Working with these guys all day was extremely easy. When Alonzo came to check on me later, I let him know that he put me in the right place. We set up a work schedule that would allow me to work forty hours a week but still make it to football practice every day. The laboratory was open twenty-four hours a day to anyone with security access, so showing up at 4 a.m. to start my shift was easy.

My biggest challenge was proving my worth to this team. If they were going to let me work unsupervised in a laboratory with millions of dollars' worth of equipment, then I had to be *great*. It was not enough to just show up early; I had to produce, especially since I was working solo for the first four hours of my shift. I proved that I was working my butt off. When they gave me a task, I would rush to get it done. When they showed up in the morning, I made sure they knew I had completed all of my work—and some of theirs too. I kept hearing that saying I grew up with: *As a black man, you gotta work twice as hard to get where you wanna go.*

I was damned proud of myself, especially so on the day when Jasen wanted to talk to me about the huge stack of circuit boards I'd soldered at my lab workstation. I smiled and stuck my chest out in a wildly triumphant fashion.

"That's good news, right?" I asked, waiting for a shower of Jasen praise.

"No, Yohancé, it's not good news. You have already done double the work we expected you to complete this summer. When we had our meeting here yesterday, while you were at football practice, Alonzo asked us why we are overworking you. You need you to slow down and not burn yourself out."

My chest deflated quickly.

"I didn't mean to make anybody look bad, or imply that you guys were slacking. I'm just really grateful to be getting paid so much money to do this job."

"Dude, you are probably making only a small fraction of what everybody else in this lab is, and you are working yourself to death."

His words did not make much sense at the time, but I trusted Jasen. So I adjusted myself.


**Football**

After a day in the lab, where I was playing grown-up, I would head to football practice, where I could finally act my age. Most of my teammates came there from summer school. Because I had to take one train and two buses, a lot of times I was late for practice and would be the last person to enter the field for stretch formation. G-Man would notice.

"Nice of you to join us, YOH-HON-SAY! Everyone take a lap around the field for YOH-HON-SAY being late to practice again!"

G-Man was relentless. And now I looked bad in front of my teammates. I didn't just switch my clothes when I came back to the hood. I had to strip away the professional accent on the gridiron. I tried to make amends as I ran alongside one of my big guys on the defensive line.

"Waddup, big James Brock! You ready to run a bit faster for the Shaw?"

"Nigga, you ready to show up on time for the Shaw?"

"Oooo, I could see you mad, but I think G-Man just wanna move all the leaders to the front of the stretch formation."

"OK, Yohancé, so you want me to run faster to grab one of those spots?"

"I mean … If you look up there, Junior, Stoney, Marcus Martin, and fat boy Antonio Loggins are already there. If we hurry, we can get the last two spots, and all the big boys can lead the stretches."

Almost all of the linemen were the same size, but whoever was the slowest would be called fat boy by the rest of the big boys.

"Marcus and them probably cheated to get they fat asses all the way up there, Yohancé. I bet they cut across the field when G-Man's back was turned."

"Brock, I betcha me and you could just sprint past everybody else and grab those spots, though."

"Aight, I'm wichu."

G-Man, clipboard in hand, surveyed the field and continued to give us a hard time.

"I see you and Brock made it to the front, YOH-HON-SAY," he said as he decided who his leaders were for the day. He turned to Marcus and pointed his clipboard at him and shouted, "How did your fat ass get to the front!?" G-Man's surprise wasn't directed at Marcus for not being a leader on the team. Marcus was actually one of the best players on the team, and a sure bet to play professional football. The reason G-Man questioned him was because Marcus was six-foot-four and weighed over 350 pounds. If Marcus and the fat boys were all in the front, then the whole team must have walked a lap, or the fat boys cheated. No one on our team ever snitched, though, so we just went on with our practice.

After several hours of drills and running—lots and lots of running—practice was over. It was time to get ready to repeat this marathon of a process. As I walked back to the locker room, G-MAN called me into his office. He told me to go shower and put my gear up first, and that he wanted to see me afterward. I had no clue what he wanted, but I always did as he told me. When I was done, I came back to his office.

"Yohancé, I need you to understand what it is I'm trying to do for you here, OK? This is mentorship, and I need to steer you in the right direction."

"I hear you, G-Man. What's up?"

"Well, it's just that you are probably making a lot of money over at that Aerospace Corporation, and I don't want you to do something stupid, like blow it all on clothes or jewelry or something."

"Ahhh. You think I care about clothes and jewelry, G-Man."

"No I never said that, YOH-HON-SAY. Don't be putting words in my mouth, now. I'm just trying to make sure you are picking up what I'm putting down here."

"I think I am, G-Man."

"Oh, are you, YOH-HON-SAY? You're telling me that my message did not go in one ear … and out the other? You are. Understanding the words. That are coming … out of my mouth?"

I was laughing inside at his attempt to get information out of me without asking any question that could be misinterpreted as overreaching. He was like a father to me. He could have just asked me directly what I was doing with my money.

Patiently, while hiding my urge to laugh, I explained to G-Man that I had a bank account, and my priority was saving all my money to buy food for my mom, little brother, and me. He listened to my words and smiled wide.

"Well that's good to hear, YOH-HON-SAY! That sounds like a plan! I think that's smart!"

I could tell G-Man was proud of me, because when he let me out of his office, he had a joyful pep in his step. He was always a happy man with a song in his heart, but I knew that my good news had cranked the volume up for him.


**Back to Work**

It was soon my last day at the Aerospace Corporation. That first summer of work flew by. I had to get a final evaluation from my boss, Alonzo Prater. He asked me to follow him down the hallway.

"You must have heard the good news, Yohancé. Come on, let's go." We were going to meet with Jim.

Jim Matsumoto was an elderly Asian man who shared duties with Alonzo as a senior engineer in charge of our lab. Together they would evaluate my performance this summer. I tensed myself for what they might say: I had built projects too fast and sometimes left work a few minutes too early. I was wrong.

"Dude, we want you back here whenever you get a break from school," Alonzo said. Jim nodded fiercely in approval.

"Yohancé, you are a very valuable asset to this team, and we are glad to have given you this opportunity," said Jim.

"That's awesome, guys. Any criticism for me? I can handle it."

"Nope. We got nothing. As a matter of fact, we've been praising you so much that the big boss wants to meet you," said Alonzo.

"The big boss?" I uttered in confusion.

"Yeah, Yohancé. The CEO of The Aerospace Corporation: Dr. Wanda Austin. I'm escorting you over to her office. Read your emails," Alonzo teased.

Soon we were crossing the vast campus, heading toward the biggest, fanciest building. After being approved by security, we climbed an intense amount of stairs. The journey through this extensive high-tech metallic building was intimidating, involving elevators and passcodes. But it helped to know that Dr. Austin wanted to meet me.

When we finally reached the top of our last flight of stairs, two employees from HR greeted us. They thanked us for being so prompt, given the CEO's last-minute request. Dr. Austin had found a small gap in her busy schedule and summoned us for a quick meeting. The whole experience felt very surreal. I was soon in her office, and I stretched my hand out to shake hers.

Dr. Austin was a middle-aged woman with stylish reading glasses and a powerfully warming smile. My first impression of her was that she was a cool grandmother.

"Good Morning, Yohancé." I couldn't believe she said my name correctly. She knew who I was.

Alonzo was laughing and slapping his knee as he stood up to join in the greetings. He couldn't contain how happy he was that this meeting was happening.

"Yohancé, this meeting has been in the works for some time now. Alonzo and I have been in discussion about you, and there are some things I need to tell you and questions I'd like to ask."

"Yes, ma'am. I'm open to receiving any wisdom you have for me."

We took our seats, and Dr. Austin told me that hiring me into the laboratory section of this multibillion-dollar corporation was a huge gamble that paid off immensely. Alonzo had convinced her of my character, and she was thrilled to have me on the team. Dr. Austin spoke about leadership, overcoming adversity, character, and becoming the best people we could be. She urged me to continue in my career development, and not to hesitate to reach out to her for anything I needed.

As Alonzo and I left her office, Dr. Austin offered one final statement to prove her commitment to my future.

"Yohancé, you're definitely going to college. I'm just trying to determine which school would be a good fit for you."

I wanted to tell her that I was going to attend the United States Air Force Academy (USAFA), but I didn't want to come off as arrogant or ungrateful. Instead, I danced around the matter, saying, "Ma'am, I think I want to go to a service academy, like West Point, Annapolis, or the United States Air Force Academy."

"The Air Force Academy is a very good school, Yohancé," Dr. Austin said.

"Yes, ma'am, that's my number-one choice."

Dr. Austin smiled as we exited her office.

# Chapter 26
## Running Away from Church

"AYE! LISTEN UP!"

Practice was over, and this loudmouthed buffoon named Shannon Penn was demanding the attention of everyone in the locker room.

"Everybody look, I need your attention! Hey!!"

The whole team was rushing out of the locker room to enjoy what we had left of our Saturday afternoon. But this player thought it was a good time to make an announcement. Seeing that Shannon was six-foot-three and 230 pounds, we listened. Plus, he was a senior, and I was just a junior at the time, in the fall of 2009.

"Alright, y'all know ya boy, Shannon Penn! And I wanna invite all y'all to come to church with me this Sunday!"

Shannon started passing out flyers to get us to commit to going to church with him. He was fast, snatching people left and right as they tried to escape the locker room without a flyer.

"You know you want this flyer, Yohancé. Jesus loves you, and he's been tryna save yo ass for a long time now!"

I almost fell over from how hard he made me laugh. I didn't have any plans for the next day, but I was still hesitant to accept his invitation.

"Shannon, I'm low-key religious, but I hate going to church. I've tried this experiment many times, and I know what the outcome will be."

"Yohancé, if you religious, then you gotta come to my church tomorrow, bro. This sermon is about to be off the chain! The pastor told me to bring everybody and they momma."

"Aight, I'll be there tomorrow, Shannon."

He was a damned good salesman.

As soon as he was done convincing me, he sprinted up to another small group and almost tackled them into their lockers. This week's sermon must have really been amazing, I thought, because he'd never had this much enthusiasm when he invited us in the past.

After I got back to *the place*, I thought about going back on my promise to show up at the church. The shelter was two hours' worth of public transportation away from Crenshaw High School. Shannon had sold a few players on how close his church was to the school, but that didn't help me one bit. I would spend two hours going and two hours coming back. Which meant I would lose four hours of my already miniscule weekend. I could use that time to study, or play piano, or just rest. In the end, I decided I had to take the journey to church to build character.

When I arrived, I found it was not very big, but it was well-kept. A decent portion of the team had showed up, all huddled in the back and awaiting direction from Shannon. I learned later that Shannon wanted to point out to his pastor how many Crenshaw Cougars he brought with him, since this was part of some competition. The church drew a strong attendance, so few pews were empty. It felt righteous to be standing in church next to men whom I'd bled, sweat, and struggled beside on the gridiron.

I thought that if there was any chance of me liking church, this would be it—but I hated it. The pastor's sermon was about manhood, and the best way for men in our community to be leaders. The subject was what I wanted to know more about, but the message was deeply flawed, and accusatory. He began his sermon speaking about promiscuity and premarital sex. I thought his judgements would be easy to shake off. I had never felt any spiritual convictions about my past endeavors, because of how strong and natural those behaviors came to me. I knew this behavior was something to be tamed, controlled; but eradicating it completely was impossible. The pastor then linked this behavior to an inferior man, and called such a man lacking in manhood. That's when he lost my respect. I was no less of a man or a leader in my community for having a relatively tame lust in my heart.

The only thing the pastor's words made me question, was his motives. He didn't make me question my faith, my character, or my manhood.

It wasn't the perceived attacks upon *my* manhood that irked me the most during that sermon. The pastor went on to attack homosexuality as an immensely grotesque behavior that was the antithesis of manhood. I was sweating and trying to understand how this man of faith had so much hatred in his heart. Even though I was not a homosexual man, some of my closest friends and mentors were, and none of them were less of a man for it. I tried to calm myself down by laughing at myself for taking the most offense at this section of the sermon. In my head, I told myself: *You're only mad because after what happened in Hollywood, you might be a little gay.* I got a chuckle out of that joke, and my temperature started to go down.

I had made up my mind to leave. When I stood up, everyone started clapping. I had gotten up just as they were calling people to the front of the church to be saved. This was yet another ritual in my religion that I had never participated in. My belief in Jesus Christ as my savior did not need the validation of man. I was already saved. But I wondered whether I was too confident, too arrogant, so I decided to walk to the front of the church rather than out the back.

Accepting Jesus Christ as my Lord and Savior in front of a crowd of almost two hundred people was easy. I just repeated the words and made sure they meant something to me. The five of us that got saved were led to the back of the church to fill out prayer cards. The card did not have enough room for what I wanted to write. I wrote a long explanation about how I am not guaranteed to eat dinner every night, and how I wanted them to pray that God showed me a way to feed my family and myself. All I wanted was their prayers.

When Shannon saw me in the hallway at school the next day, he dashed in my direction and gave me an envelope.

"Sister Stanly told me to give this to you."

"Thank you, Shannon!"

I waited until he walked away to open the envelope, because I was so horrible at receiving gifts. The envelope had money and a message. The message, written on yellow paper, told me how happy the churchgoers were that I got saved that Sunday. Multiple people signed it and said they would honor my request and pray for me.

The cash was charity. I knew I would have difficulty spending it, so I walked over to this tall, skinny black kid in the hallway. He had dark black skin, jet-black eyes, and a funny-looking big nose. This freshman with curly dark hair and a nonchalant air of confidence about him was the perfect candidate to take this unwanted money off my hands. All the money in the world seemed to gravitate toward this kid anyhow.

"Niglet, stick your hand out."

"What for?"

"Just do it."

He opened his hand, and I slapped the money into his palm.

"Thank you!" Kumasi yelled across the hall as I turned to walk to my next class. I waved off his thanks, grateful to get rid of that burden. I would never go back to that church again.

# Chapter 27
## A Traveler's Perspective

FOR THE FIRST few seconds, I just didn't know where I was. There were bright lights shooting down a long corridor, and the floor seemed to be shaking like I was in an earthquake. There were rows of chairs in pairs of two with no one in them. Giant windows to my left and right gave me no information, as a black abyss stared back at me in a sort of reflection. My head was whirling slowly in circles as I tried to wake up from what I thought must be a dream. But it wasn't a dream. I was close to my exit, and even though the sun had yet to rise, it was time for me to get up and exit the bus.

Kumasi and I had this ability to snooze on the back of the city bus and wake up right as the bus came to our stop. We would slide like zombies out of our seats and exit the back door. By then we were fully awake and ready for the next bus or train on our journey to school.

We would ride one bus for about forty-five minutes south, then grab another that took us a few minutes east, and we would zig-zag our way through the city. The whole process was very tedious, but we had perfected it.

"Now approaching Crenshaw and Slauson."

However, if we ever heard this automated message over the loud-speaker, it was a sure bet that we had accidentally passed our stop. This intersection was not far from Crenshaw High, though, so we could easily walk back a few blocks and blend in with neighborhood kids walking to school.

Kumasi and I almost never rode the bus together on our way back up to *the place*. He would be in basketball or water polo practice, and neither one of us ever wanted to wait on one another. Without him as an extra set of ears, I frequently missed my stops while riding public transportation. Sometimes I would catch up to Kumasi and find him sleeping at a train stop, where he had obviously missed several rides.

There was a man who rode almost every bus and train that I did, and his face was starting to become familiar to me. I noticed that he would ride all the way up to the Valley from the Crenshaw area, but I didn't feel like he was following me. He was a black man, about six feet tall, and had an average build. His eyeglasses had metal frames, and his goatee made him look about thirty. But one day I took a closer look at him on the bus and realized he was my age. I had to find out more about this strange man.

"Hello there! My name is Yohancé. Rhymes with Beyo—"

"Yeah, I know who you are, Yohancé. We go to the same school, and you're one of those football players everyone is always talking about. My name is Timothy Brown, and it's nice to finally meet you."

"Timothy, it's good to meet you too. I just thought it was a bit strange how I see you on this bus almost every day and you actually ride it to the end of the line just like me."

"Yohancé, you see me every morning too; you just don't remember me," Timothy said with a chuckle.

I thought he had to be lying, because I have an impeccable memory and I could not remember seeing him on my ride to school. He only existed on my ride back to *the place*.

"Are you sure you are not mistaking me for someone else?" I asked him.

"Dude, you are hard to mistake, with that huge black duffle bag you carry, and how aggressively you march to the back of the bus. I usually sit in the very front, and you walk right past me."

"Is that right, Timothy?"

"Yeah man. You and your little brother take the back seats and sprawl out like y'all ain't never slept a day in ya lives."

"So, Timothy, riddle me this. Why is it that you are on the bus at four in the morning to be able to observe this whole thing?"

I thought he might be homeless too.

"Yohancé, I just like riding the bus. I get on 'em early and stay on 'em late. I can't get enough of it."

When I heard him say that, I thought this guy must be crazy. I had a thousand more questions for him, because his brain clearly worked differently than mine. Riding the bus made him happy and gave him a sense of adventure. He knew all of the bus drivers on our route to school and always sat in the very front in order to talk to the driver about how awesome their job was. All Timothy ever wanted to do was drive that bus. It turns out he was not homeless like me. He just chose to spend time at his auntie or grandmother's house in the Valley, which afforded him more time on the bus.

I got closer to Timothy. Sometimes when he got off the bus, I would exit with him. Over a burger we could continue our conversation. I didn't think he was smarter than me, but he was certainly a lot wiser. I thought it was my duty to reach for all the gold and accolades I could get my hands on in life, but Timothy showed me how wrong I was. I questioned him over and over again about how he could be at his happiest if he were a bus driver for the rest of his life. Both of my parents had their post-graduate degrees, and yet after all that education, they met each other as bus drivers. They *chose* to be bus drivers. I never understood why they chose to drive a bus rather than run a company; they never told me. Timothy Brown seemed like the only one who could connect these puzzle pieces for me, and I yearned for his wisdom.

"Yohancé, it's actually kinda simple. Stop comparing yourself to everyone else, and just do what makes you happy. Success and happiness are very personal, and you don't need anyone else's permission to feel good about yourself."

I would never forget his words to me that day.

To me, everything is a competition. But Timothy believed that success wasn't only about striving to be the CEO of a big company or President of the United States. Timothy believed that success is a personal thing that can only be measured by how happy you are in your life. How he saw life and career was completely different from my perspective. I would have to shift my paradigm extensively to even come close to his way of life—something I knew I would struggle with for a long time.

This man was going to be a bus driver, and there would be almost nothing I could accomplish that would ever make me more successful than him. He did not tell me that last part; I came to that conclusion on my own. I needed to be more like Timothy and find happiness in my life.

My first step toward being more like Timothy was dropping this tough guy persona when I got on the bus. Acting angry made me angry, and I was done with all that. I started sitting in the front of the bus and engaging in conversation with folks instead of sleeping or giving people the stink eye. One of the coolest people I met after I changed my attitude was a man named Mr. Early. He drove the early city bus down Crenshaw Boulevard, and his wife was a teacher at my school. Mr. Early had a thousand pieces of advice to give anyone who would listen. His bald head would shine in the sunlight, as he turned the big steering wheel. Because I had opened myself to the world, he and I had very long and deep conversations. Soon I began to trust him with information that I seldom shared with anyone, the type of info you don't give till you think you're on your deathbed. Mr. Early urged me to go meet his wife; he said they both would support me in any way I needed. They wanted to have a hand in helping me reach my dreams.

I grew to trust Mr. and Mrs. Early very much; they were the first people to read my personal statement for college admissions. I handed it to Mr. Early one day when I got on the bus and explained what it was.

"What are you calling your personal statement, Yohancé? Like, what's the title?"

"I like to call it UPOV, which I pronounce, you-pove, Mr. Early."

"Oh yeah? What does that mean, exactly?"

"UPOV is a funky acronym for Underprivileged Overachiever."

"I like that a lot. I hope you told these colleges the full story, so those doors swing open for you."

"Mr. Early, I've never told anyone the full story, and I don't know that I ever plan to."

"Well you never know, Yohancé. This essay may just be the start of all that."

# Chapter 28
## Let's Eat

WHEN TIMES GOT tough, I would usually just sweep all my problems under the rug. G-Man had given me eight extra lockers in the football locker room, so I had plenty of space to hide my problems. I thought I'd made a lot of money at the Aerospace Corporation, so I was surprised when it ran out. In truth, the salary was more than double what my peers made that summer, but I never properly calculated how expensive it was to feed and take care of my family. I had to start revising my priorities, and that meant abandoning some responsibilities. The first one I dropped was getting money together to wash everyone's clothes. I had enough donated clothes that I thought I wouldn't have to wash them too frequently. I'd just pile all my dirty clothes in my eight lockers and wait for an opportunity to hand-wash them when everyone left the locker room.

G-Man began to get complaints about the smell from my lockers. He realized my problem. G-Man had offered me help in a myriad of ways, but I always turned him down and told him I was just grateful to be able to play on his team. This time he did not ask to help me, though. He told me what was about to go down. G-Man opened up all my lockers and told me to throw my dirty clothes in a bag. He was going to wash my clothes and bring them all back to me tomorrow. He was not asking, so there was nothing to say no to. When G-Man told me to do something—I did it.

I don't think G-Man ever confided in the rest of the coaching staff as to what the full details of my predicament were. Many of my coaches tried to use the same motivations on me that they used with the rest of my teammates ... until they found something that really worked.


During practice the next day, Coach Bear Claw was getting frustrated with how the linemen would not be aggressive toward one another, so he set up a drill to remedy the situation. I was still not giving it my best, though. As a consequence, Coach Bear Claw sent me to run around the field before returning to his drill.

"Yohancé, why are you being so soft today? You know what, man? *Go take a lap!*"

When I returned, I found that Coach Bear Claw had enlisted the assistant head coach, Coach Sash, to help him. Both of these coaches were large men with the stature of a professional NFL lineman, but Coach Sash was always a bit more intimidating. He was a Creole man with a deep voice and a pronounced lisp. He rarely spoke, but if he did, it was a sure bet that someone was messing up and was about to be punished.

I returned to the drill with a little more enthusiasm this time, though fear was never my biggest motivator. The drill was simple: two people grabbed hold of a tackle dummy from opposite sides. When the whistle blew, they fought to get control of it. In full pads and helmets, nothing was off limits. The point of the drill was to instill more aggression and fight into the linemen. Coach Bear Claw wanted the offensive linemen to hate the defensive linemen so that we would practice harder against each other.

When Coach Bear Claw called me up to the front, I knew he must have some sort of trick up his sleeve. Instead of calling one of the fat boys to pair up with me, he selected one of my fellow defensive linemen, Junior Alexis. Coach Bear Claw was snickering in the background, as if he knew something I didn't. Junior was this huge dark-skinned Haitian boy with the strength of ten men, but he was not much stronger than me. He wouldn't be able to overpower me. I knew Coach Bear Claw would only be disappointed when he saw us in a stalemate.

After struggling for what felt like an eternity, with neither of us gaining any ground, Coach Sash stepped in and told us to stop. He reiterated the purpose of the drill and told us to think outside the box in terms of ways to be aggressive. Right before Junior and I could reset in the drill, a large group of linebackers and other players on the team formed a crowd to watch the fight. Coach Bear Claw immediately told Junior and me to break contact so that he could change the drill slightly. Instead of fighting Junior, I was now going to be facing one of the most aggressive players on the team: our star middle linebacker, Ronald Stovall aka "The 38-Special." He was the type of player who kept a tally of how many people he sent to the hospital every season. He tackled with zero remorse for human life and loved to watch our opponents get taken off the field in a stretcher. As long as he didn't fight dirty, I could win. But he always fought dirty.

I heard the whistle blow, and I tightened my arms around the bag. Instead of trying to wrestle the bag out of my arms, The 38-Special dropped the bag and punched me directly in my chin. I didn't even know it was physically possible to punch someone under their helmet like that. When I threw my hands up to catch my balance, Ronald snatched the bag and held it over his head like a trophy. The crowd started to cheer, and Coach Bear Claw slapped himself in frustration. Ronald wasn't just a dirty fighter, he was creative. Coach Bear Claw reset the drill and issued me a small threat, as if running a few laps would motivate me to fight like The 38-Special. The whistle blew again, and this time Ronald sweep-kicked me and dropped an elbow on my back. He wrapped the bag between his legs and started to choke me on the ground before the coaches blew the whistle to end the drill.

"Coach Bear Claw, I think you're not giving Yohancé the right motivation here," said Coach Sash.

"Is that right, Yohancé!? Do you need something to motivate you to not be so soft?" Coach Bear Claw shouted.

I was too busy trying to catch my breath to respond. I wondered if the linebackers tried to hurt each other this bad at every practice.

"Well, Yohancé, I'll tell you what. If you beat Ronald at this drill, you can have my burger at the end of practice. That big, juicy burger you saw me put in the fridge is yours if you win."

I wanted that burger so bad, but I didn't know how I was going to beat The 38-Special. In order to win, I had to try to hurt Ronald.

This time when the whistle blew, I dropped to my butt and sweep-kicked Ronald with both legs. When he fell, I rolled back to my feet and tucked the bag under my left arm. I stood over him searching menacingly for an opening. Ronald held on to the other end of the bag as I struck him over and over again in his back. I punched him sixteen times before Coach Bear Claw pulled me off of The 38-Special.

Apparently, the whistle had blown a long time ago, and the only one holding on to the tackling bag was me.

"Yohancé, we get it. The burger is yours already. Damn! You can't be trying to hurt everybody after the whistle," said Coach Bear Claw with a huge smirk on his face.

There was no bad blood between Ronald and me, but there was definitely a murderous look in his eyes after that drill. Maybe that was how the linebackers hurt so many people on game day. They took out all their frustrations on whatever team we played that week. I actually felt sorry for the team we had to play next.

**Game Time**

The Team Captains Meeting

It was a Friday night, and every seat in our stands was filled. The crowd had come to see the hardest-hitting football team in Los Angeles. Before the game could kick off, there was a bit of a formality to take care of: the coin toss. It never really mattered who got the ball first, but for some reason we always preferred to play defense initially. Coach Bear Claw was selecting which one of the captains to send to the coin toss, and I noticed he was only picking big men that game.

"Coach Bear Claw, can I go represent the team for the coin toss?"

It was a long shot, but I figured he might let me act like I was one of the captains.

"Sure, Yohancé. The coin toss is just a mind game. Let Marcus do all the talking, and you just stand there, looking mean the whole time."

"I got it, Coach," I said as I sprinted over to meet the other captains.

Marcus looked at the rest of his captains and addressed us like we were about to go to war.

"Aye, bros, don't be smiling at nobody and mess this shit up. Especially you, Yohancé. We all gotta look ready to fight!"

I knew how to put on my game face.

When our four captains met the other team's four captains, I got to see firsthand just how important this part of the game was. Their quarterback was chubby and looked frightened as the four massive linemen walked toward him. Standing at my side was fat boy slim Marcus Martin, lil bus James Brock, and man child Junior Alexis.

"OK, gentlemen. I want a nice, clean game from both of ya," the referee declared.

"When you score today, act like you got some sense and you've been there before."

I wondered why the referee said that to us. None of the big men at the coin toss had ever scored a touchdown, and it was highly unlikely that today would be the day.

The coin toss went the home team's way, and The Shaw decided as we always did.

"You guys get ball first," Marcus said with a sinister look on his face.

As we walked away from the coin toss, the big men let out their excitement.

"They got no idea!" shouted Brock. "That team is about to get *murdered* by this wild pack of nig—"

"Brock! It ain't even that serious, bruh!" I chimed in.

"Hey man … I'm just sayin'. It ain't even 'bout to be close. We all 'bout to eat."

Brock was right. It was not even the end of the second quarter yet, and this was clearly going to be another blow-out. We were already winning by more than thirty points, so it made no sense to me why we were still tormenting the other team. Only half of the starting lineup had been replaced by their back-ups, and we were still scoring every time we touched the ball. When it was time for the defense to get back on the field, I strapped up my helmet and sprinted into the game for the first time that night. The ball was snapped to start the play, and I got run over by a bunch of offensive linemen as the running back trotted on by me. He didn't get far, though, because our middle linebackers—Hayes Pullard and The 38-Special—collided with the runner in a devastating blow. The running back tried to run between our linebackers, and as they laid him out, there was a tremendous "Crack!" that sounded like a gunshot. I was used to hearing this noise, because that's how it always sounded when The 38-Special tackled somebody. This time, though, I could not tell who did more damage, Hayes or Ronald. That running back stayed down for a long time, spread-eagle on the turf. I was proud of my team, and just a little happy that I contributed to that tackle by beating up Ronald in practice that week.

Our defensive coordinator was not happy with me, though. Coach Doe called the whole team over to the sidelines while the boy on the ground received medical treatment. The first thing the coach did was yell at me for lying on the ground.

"Yohancé, don't be missing any tackles out there! That one should have been yours!"

"I got the next one, Coach Doe!"

We took a quick water break while the kid got back to his feet, and eventually the referee said we could play again. The rest of the team was already running back to the field, but Coach Doe told me to stay back for a bit. When all the other players were far enough away, Coach Doe spoke to me privately, saying, "If you sack that quarterback, I'll buy you a steak dinner at a fancy restaurant." As he said it, Coach Bear Claw began shaking his head.

The next play, I sprinted faster than I'd ever gone before. I moved so fast I thought I must have cheated the snap. But when I reached the quarterback, he had the ball, so I lifted him up and slammed him into the turf. There was no penalty, and I had done nothing wrong, but they told me to get off the field. I was confused. Apparently, I was the one who'd hurt someone this time, and we had to run back to the sidelines while the guy received medical treatment.

Coach Bear Claw looked at Coach Doe in disappointment and shock as he said, "Man, I told you what Yohancé did to Ronald for a burger! Why would you offer him a steak to hurt that boy? This one is all your fault."

Fortunately, the quarterback got up soon.

Coach Doe looked at Coach Bear Claw and said, "I take responsibility for my actions. You cain't be soft in this sport. At least they know what to expect when they come 'round here now."

Coach Doe stuck his chest out and added, "Them Crenshaw boys is tryna eat!"

"Literally!"

# Chapter 29
## Checking in with Mom

FOOTBALL GAMES AT Crenshaw High always seemed to last late into the night. When the clock finally ran out, all the players would line up for an end-of-game ritual. Both home and visitor teams formed lines to walk past each other, congratulating one another on the game. Before I joined the team, I expected this ceremony to be full of angst and spite.

I was wrong.

Players would congratulate an opponent that gave them a really hard tackle or intercepted their pass during the game. We would tell them how much fun it was competing against them. These big, muscular men were stopping to hug one another and wish each other well in the rest of their season. There was this sort of post-game comradery with your opponents that made you think, "Since you guys beat us, you better go on to beat everybody else just as bad, or worse."

When we finished our exhibition of good sportsmanship, we'd head to the locker room to hear G-Man give a speech. Usually G-Man would let us go a little crazy in the locker room as we celebrated our win. He would then tell us to calm down and humble ourselves so that he could deliver a message of wisdom. That was my favorite part of a football game—The G-Man speech at the end. Toward the end of his speech, G-Man would brief us about next week's opponent and Saturday practice. G-Man always ended with the Lord's Prayer, to remind us what a blessing it was to play such a great sport.

No one wanted to be the last one out of the locker room, because that person would usually be held responsible for cleaning up after everyone else. A lot of the boys didn't even take a shower after the game, citing that they would just get into their parents' car stinking and shower when they got home. I was always the slug of the group, as I took my time showering and getting ready to leave the locker room. None of the players really knew why I would move so slowly, but I definitely had my reasons. I did not want them to see me walk to the back of the locker room and open all six of my extra lockers. I was really good with numbers and had all my combinations memorized, but I didn't want my teammates thinking I had these lockers because I was privileged.

It would be late in the evening when I finally emerged from the locker room. Most of the coaches and parents would be gone by now, making the place a ghost town. Before leaving, teammates often offered me a bed to sleep in at their house, but I almost always turned it down. I think G-Man told the boys to keep asking me every week. But my responsibilities to my family came first.

Someone was waiting for me by the concession stand, and I didn't want to keep her there all night. The concession stands sold a lot of food during our games, but there would almost always be leftovers. When I turned the corner to see rows and rows of sandwiches wrapped in aluminum foil and stacked on a few tables, I knew we had hit the jackpot. Standing behind these tables was a pretty lady with long, wavy hair, wood-brown skin, and mystically gorgeous eyes. She was staring into a small space above her head, where I thought she might be daydreaming about catching butterflies again.

"Hi, Mom. How was it working the concession stands again this week?"

"Oh, hi, Ajamu! Where did you come from? Really snuck up on me there, didn't you!"

"I don't think I'm capable of sneaking up on anyone right now, Mom," I said, nodding to the ice packs wrapped around my arms and legs.

"I see. I see. Are you hurt, Ajamu?"

"Just preventative sports treatment, Mom. I'm a little banged up, but I'll be all right. How was your night?"

"My night was fantastic! I was serving people and really helping out, you know? We sold a bunch of stuff, but I guess we still never ran out. G-Man said we could have all the stuff that's left over."

"That's really kind of him, Mom. I think I have enough space for all of it in my duffle bag."

"Do we really need all of this food though, Ajamu? I mean ... it's just a lot."

"Mom, I need every single burger, hot dog, and condiment on this table. Whatever does not fit into our mini-fridge, I will eat tonight. The more we take now, the better our chances at not starving this week."

"OK, go ahead, honey. I just thought it was a bit excessive."

Being constantly hungry made me an angry person, which is why I dug in my heels. But I did not want to show any attitude to my mother, so I just changed the subject.

"Mom, did you watch much of the game this time?"

"Oh ... yeah, I did watch for a bit this time. I think I'm starting to understand this whole football thing now."

"Is that so, Mom?"

"Yeah! So, when you guys have the ball, you are trying to score. And when the other team has the ball, they are trying to score. Right? I think it's called a touchdown when you score."

"That's pretty much the whole game, Mom. You got it all figured out now." The way she explained football made me feel so lighthearted and happy.

"What exactly do people mean when they say stuff like 'he 'bout to eat' or 'he laid the wood'? Those kinds of phrases confuse me, Ajamu."

"Mom, when people say 'lay the wood,' they mean you gave a really hard tackle. And 'eating' is just a universal term for doing well at any part of football."

"I guess that makes sense. Are you really good at this sport, Ajamu?"

I laughed when she asked that, because it could not be further from the truth.

"No, Mom, I'm actually not very good at the sport, and I'm lucky if I get to contribute to my team's success."

"But the announcer called your name several times over the loud-speaker. I think you even got a touchdown today. That kind of confused me because I thought you were on defense."

"I just got a few good plays and got really lucky by picking up the ball in the end zone after a guy dropped it. That was probably the only time I'll ever score."

"One of the times when they called your name, the crowd started screaming really loud. Do you remember that? This guy in the stands started yelling, 'You can't stop this ass whoopin'!'"

"Yeah, I remember that. I think that was my robotics teacher, Mr. Pelligrin. He played football for Stanford, and he gets really hyper at our games."

"I'm just glad that I can be here to help support you too, Ajamu. I love you."

"I love you too, Mom. What are your plans for the rest of the night?"

"I'm staying at a friend's house down here. Were you planning on riding the bus back up to the shelter tonight?"

"I gotta get some of this food to Kumasi and store the rest in the fridge."

"But what if you miss the last bus for the night up in the Valley?"

"Then I'll walk the rest of the way, Mom."

"Ajamu, that's a mighty long walk."

"I guess I better not miss the bus then, Mom. Peace."

"Peace."

# Chapter 30
## A Bad Day at the Shaw

THERE WAS NEVER a clock at practice, and watches and cell phones were forbidden. There was no regular schedule that let the players know when practice was over. The sun had gone down hours ago, but the exact time was a mystery to everyone except G-Man. Most coaches kept their watch in their pocket and seldom checked the time anyhow. Even the assistant coaches were not allowed to tell the players what time it was.

Today was different, though. We expected to practice very late because we had been invited to play one final game at the state championship. Our opponent was De La Salle, a legendary football team. They held the title for the longest-winning streak of any high school football program in the nation: 12 years, 151 games, 0 losses.

Even with the insurmountable task of beating this team ahead of us, this particular night's practice felt excessively long. It was a cold night, and it felt like even a late practice should have ended two or three hours ago. A small group of us on the sidelines approached coach Coach Bear Claw to ask why practice was not over yet, but he looked as confused as us. Eventually we convinced Coach Bear Claw to ask G-Man if practice was going to be much longer. None of the players wanted to catch the smackdown by questioning G-Man's methods. When Coach Bear Claw returned, he didn't offer any specifics. So we continued to practice through the night, until G-Man's marathon of a practice ended.

Eventually practice did end, and G-Man called us all over to the sideline. We took a knee, like we always did, and waited for some G-Man wisdom. Even in the dead of night, G-Man never took off his aviator sunglasses. So when he removed them tonight, we knew something was wrong.

"Men, it's very late in the night, and I kept you all here for a very good reason. Sure, we need to run over these plays and prepare for this state championship, but there is something a little more to it tonight. I needed to keep all of you off the streets and safe on this football field for as long as I could. There is a lot going on outside of Crenshaw High School tonight, and I didn't want any of you to have a part in it. You will probably figure out more details at school tomorrow, but for now I will share with you what I know. One of your classmates was killed in a car accident as he walked across Crenshaw Boulevard. Many of you may have known this boy, and we are going to take the time to pray for him and his family here shortly. His name was Garrette Wheeler and ..."

"Garrette!?" said one of my teammates.

"Garrette Wheeler!?" said a second teammate.

We never interrupted G-Man, so these outbursts felt strange. But G-Man allowed it. I didn't know who this kid was, but the growing chorus of chatter made me think the whole football team knew him. I just shook my head cluelessly as everyone started talking about this kid. One of the wide receivers on the team, number eighteen, gave me a funny look and told me I did know Garrette Wheeler. I looked him dead in the eye and told him I had no idea who Garrette Wheeler was. I was happy to not know him, too, because I was one of the only players who left the field without tears in my eyes.

When we got out of the locker room, we learned all of the parents had come to pick up my teammates. I tried to sneak away to catch the bus, but apparently Garrette Wheeler had died at my bus stop, so G-Man would not allow me to take that bus tonight. G-Man told me to get into the car with our star linebacker, Hayes Pullard, and that he would take me where I needed to go.

Hayes was one of the few players with his own car, but he looked so tired from the long practice that I was hesitant to ride with him. I contemplated asking him to just allow me to spend the night at his house, but he and I were not close friends. Because I couldn't let the whole team know I was homeless, I never let anyone hang too close to me outside of football practice.

Hayes had the air conditioning on full blast and pointed directly at his face as he leaned into his steering wheel and fought to stay awake. He was too tired to talk, so I just sat in the front seat nervously watching him as he drove. Hayes would drop his head or forget to open his eyes after blinking, but he never passed out. Instead of asking for him to drive the full two hours to the shelter, I asked him to drop me off at the nearby train station. I was afraid for Hayes's safety. When I got out of the car, the first thing I did was pray for Hayes to have a safe journey home. I didn't think the Shaw could stomach losing two Cougars in one night.

All my worries and prayer on Hayes's behalf were so draining that I fell asleep at the train station and missed my train. I woke up several hours later, hunched over on a bench. The smell of pee filled the air. I had not noticed just how filthy the place was. I was using my duffle bag as a pillow, and I was comfortable in this dirty train station.

At that moment, I thought about my friend Timothy Brown, who taught me that the ultimate goal was to be happy. If I could be happy being a bum who sleeps in train stations, I wouldn't have to get up to take the next train. I could just lie here all night and forget about going to school the next day. All I had to do was lower my bar of expectations and accept where I was at. It was so very tempting to just give up and call this my finish line, but something deep inside me wouldn't let me be happy down there.

*Get up, and get on the train now, Yohancé!*

"God! I'm moving! Shit!" No one else was around to hear me talk to myself, so I actually replied out loud. When I finally got up to the Valley, I found out that the buses were no longer running. Instead of taking a marathon walk to the shelter, I decided to sit down on the floor of the train station. I got right next to an outlet and started charging my phone in preparation for the next day. I decided to map out a new route to avoid the intersection where that kid got killed. I didn't look up any details to this death, because I just didn't care; I'd already forgotten his name. I just didn't want to see his blood or brains strewn across the pavement in the morning.

When I got back to the Shaw, I was dead tired.

Everyone was mourning the death of that kid. But hanging my head low from exhaustion made me look as sad as everyone else. We looked like a school full of zombies, and I was almost ready to make a joke about us before

I watched so many people break down into tears as they walked the halls. It confused me that so many people knew him, but I didn't. Maybe a lot of the people were just sensitive to the fact that he was a kid at our school and he died so tragically. I didn't have the answer to their pain, but I knew that no one was ready to laugh today.

My first class of the day was Advanced Placement English Literature, and by the looks of everyone's faces, only half of my class knew the dead kid. One classmate suggested we talk about what we were feeling. My instructor, Ms. Hanson, was happy to lead the discussion. First, she told the story of what happened last night. Apparently a car ran through an intersection in front of the school and hit four kids in the crosswalk. One kid succumbed to his injuries and died on the scene—Garrette Wheeler. She told us that Garrette was in the Gifted Magnet program, just one grade below. Our program included the top twenty-five smartest kids in every grade year, and we all usually knew each other. If Garrette Wheeler was one year below me, then I had to know who he was.

Our instructor then turned on the projector to show us a picture of Garrette. I stared at the screen in disbelief. This curly-haired, fair-skinned boy with this huge goofy smile and braces was staring back at me, almost daring me to forget his name again. There had to be a mistake, because I had told so many people that I didn't know him, and yet it could not be any further from the truth. Our instructor invited anyone to share a memory of Garrette Wheeler, so I raised my hand. When I reached the podium in the front, I thought about telling the classroom a modified story to make myself look good. But I could only muster up the truth. I told them how much of a dick I was for refusing to learn this kid's name, even after knowing him for at least four years since middle school. He looked up to me, and I knew it. He'd ask me a lot of questions about what to expect in his classes the coming year. I wasn't a total dick, I guess; I would hug him whenever I saw him in the hallway. Just a few days ago I had hugged him for giving me a discount on food he was selling out of his backpack, and I laughed in his face about still not remembering his name. Garrette Wheeler was an awesome friend, but I never knew his name until he died.

Garrette Wheeler
8–12–94 to 12–3–09
The friend I will never forget.

When I was done sharing, I walked out of the classroom. I refused to cry in front of that many people. I needed to deal with this mountain of emotions sitting on my chest. I wandered the halls with my box of tissues. But just before lunchtime I headed for the music room, where I could use a piano to flush some of this sorrow out of my heart. The choir director, Ms. Stevenson, loved me and would let me play any of the eight pianos in her classroom whenever I wanted. When I showed up at her door, she would kick people out of her room, telling them, "Y'all need to go next door with all that so Yohancé can come in here and play piano in silence." She would eat her lunch and be entranced by whatever tune I played. I thought it must annoy her to hear me play the same few songs over and over, but she never complained. Her music room was the right place to be.

None of the songs I knew could express how sad I felt, so I made up my own song that day. I knew the music would not sound as angelic as Beethoven or Mozart, but this was supposed to be therapeutic, not some grand concert. I danced my fingers around the piano keys to find notes that sounded anything like the way I felt. I discovered that the black keys south of middle C were suitable for expressing my emotions. It was so easy to play, and it actually sounded amazing. I called my masterpiece "Black Key Lament," and I played it for what felt like an eternity. There were no defined parameters to which keys I played, so recreating that song would be impossible. My heart still hurt from losing my friend, but I took solace in knowing that on my worst day I made my best music.

# Chapter 31
# A Good Day at the Shaw

EVERY GOOD DAY started off with a checklist of goals to accomplish. Some days it felt like I had to accomplish a hundred tasks in order to call my day complete. They say that there's only twenty-four hours in a day. But when you skip sleep, you can roll two days together and use forty-eight hours to stay productive. That's how I was accomplishing all my goals in one day—by cheating.

Zero period was the starting line to my marathon of tasks. Every other day of the week, the football team would meet before the start of school to lift weights and run drills. The football season was over, but we were already preparing for next year's opponents. G-Man would make sure we were good and tired before he let us leave the gym to go to our academics.

Classes were only an hour or so long. Being in the Gifted Magnet program meant that almost all of my classes were honors or Advanced Placement courses. This fast-paced learning environment stretched my mind. I was hustlin' in the more difficult subjects, such as calculus, physics, chemistry, and economics. I leaned heavily on my peers to aid me in studying, but individual tests meant I would succeed or fail on my own merits. Even though I always wanted to do better than all of my peers, especially Rodney, I never denied them assistance. That core group of students in Gifted Magnet grew very close over the years, especially as our numbers shrank. We'd lost a few students, like Kolmus, to school transfers. A few had family issues that caused them to drop out of school. None of us wanted to see each other fail, so we did everything short of cheating to raise one another up.

Lunch break at school was a marathon of its own, as I'd race against time to hang with friends who belonged to different groups in different corners of the school. All of them were special to me, so I would make every effort to see them. First, I would check in with the chess club, where I'd confidently proclaimed myself to be team captain.

"Yohancé, you know you suck at chess, right? What makes you think you are the captain of this team?"

"Eric, I'm the captain, because I said so. I may not be the best, but I am the most persistent. I will chase your ass around the board all day until I get a checkmate. That's why I'm the captain."

After leaving my nerdier friends, I'd grab food from the cafeteria and sit with the jocks on the football and basketball teams. Then I either went to the music room to play the piano or hang with classmates in the Gifted Magnet program.

Soaring Over Every Obstacle

Once school was over, track and field practice filled the first half of my afternoon. I'd run, jump, and throw things in the hot sun, until I was too tired to compete anymore. I was decent at this sport, but I was never very good at any one particular event. There were more than seven events that I competed in, and only once had I placed first. Still, I boasted the highest number of medals on my neck, as I'd taken third, fourth, or fifth place almost every time. I wore my medals with pride, chest puffed out, as I walked around the Shaw.

The robotics team filled the rest of my afternoons and late evenings. I used every bit of my popularity around the school to steal kids from other after-school programs and bring them to the robotics team. A few times I had to strong-arm my track and field buddies, but my best tool was always a story about my summer internship. Everyone—even a few teachers—wondered how *I* got a job at the Aerospace Corporation. I always gave them the same answer.

"You gotta know a guy." And that guy for me was Tim Wright.

You remember that young Santa Claus-lookin' white dude who shuffled senior engineers in front of me? Yeah, well that guy never went away. Every day after leaving work at the Corporation, Tim would spend five hours in our small robotics room facilitating our team's progress. The man was a saint. And somehow he could get high school kids jobs at the Aerospace Corporation. So far I was the only one, but it was still possible.

Toward the end of a late night in the robotics room, our adult mentors—Mr. Pelligrin, Mr. Reyes, and Tim Wright—would start shuttling kids home. Kumasi and I always stayed until the very end. At that time, the adults would contemplate who would drive us more than two hours away to the shelter. Once they learned we were taking the bus late at night, they never let us leave without a ride. The person who usually insisted on driving us was Tim Wright.

## My Big, White Dad: Tim Wright

"Yohancé, Kumasi, you boys hungry?" Tim asked as he twisted his neck over to look at us in the backseat of the car. Tim had been driving through late-night traffic in Los Angeles for more than an hour and yet somehow his generosity never waned.

"Hell yeah we hungry, Tim! But we was never gunna ask you for nuthin'. We are very grateful just to be getting a ride home right now," I said. I had learned to voice how grateful I was when I lived with Kolmus and his family. I knew I was not very good at showing how appreciative I was, because otherwise I would never have been kicked out of my buddy's house. I would not let a false spirit of entitlement rob me of what few blessings I had, especially if it meant Kumasi would suffer.

"Yohancé, I can hear your stomach growling all the way up here. You've basically been shouting at me to feed you this whole time."

Kumasi burst into laughter at Tim's joke, but I felt a bit embarrassed. Here I was trying to be grateful for whatever favors Tim did for us, and my stomach had been shouting at him this whole time.

"Tim, I—"

"Don't worry about it," Tim chuckled. "My boys gotta eat!"

"Thanks, Tim," Kumasi said.

"It's nothing, boys, it's nothing. So, you boys want Taco Bell again tonight?"

Tim knew exactly what we wanted, even if we were too shy to ask him for it. As we drove to Taco Bell, I told him a story about our father, who had passed away. My father, Abidala, always wanted his sons to speak like men. He would have us stick out our chest and speak clearly with some bass in our voice. One of his favorite places to take his sons to practice speaking like a man was Taco Bell.

"Tell him what you want, boy! Speak like a man!" my father would shout at Kumasi.

"I would like a Mexican pizza with no meat," Kumasi would whisper.

"Use your nuts, boy! Speak up! He caint hear you!"

My father never allowed us to laugh at one another when he was teaching us a lesson, so, instead, I stood next to Kumasi fighting back tears of laughter. I would tease Kumasi for the rest of his life about using his nuts to speak like a man, but now was not the time.

In Kumasi's defense, he was speaking at a decent volume, but the cashier really could not hear him. We lived in the hood, and this particular

Taco Bell had thick bulletproof glass between the staff and the costumers. Needless to say, the niglet was at a disadvantage. My father ended up ordering for Kumasi that day because there was a growing crowd, and what was meant to be a public life lesson was slowly turning into mild child abuse.

At the second register standing next to my father was a cool cat with an afro who nodded in Kumasi's direction as if he approved of my father's parenting.

My father looked in this man's direction and said, "I'm tryna teach the boy how to put some bass in his voice and speak like a man. Know what I'm sayin', brutha?"

The tough-lookin' cool cat with the afro looked at my father and replied in the squeakiest voice I have ever hear from a man, "Yeahhh … You gotta speak like a man, ma brutha!"

Tim Wright loved that story, and now he understood why I was yelling and snickering at Kumasi to use his nuts when we were at Taco Bell the other night. Now it was a chorus of Tim and me telling Kumasi to speak up as he ordered his food at the counter. After Kumasi ordered, it was my turn to step up and tell the nice lady what I wanted. My father only ever let us order two items, but Tim had told me to get whatever I wanted. I walked up to the counter and looked over the huge menu. I put my hand on my mouth and twisted my head back to look at Tim one last time.

"Dad, are you sure I can get *ANYTHING* I want?"

"Yes, son. Whatever you want it's yours," Tim replied.

The lady at the register had her mouth open and was staring at the two of us in disbelief. But in that moment, Tim Wright was my dad. And I was his boy.

# Section 4 / Fourth Quarter

Running toward a shifting finish line.

*At the end is where I need to run the hardest!*

# Chapter 32
## Ajamu Is Still My Name

IT WAS A sunny California spring morning that first day of the big robotics competition. Kumasi, Tim Wright, and I were in front of Crenshaw High School waiting for a yellow school bus to load up with our robotics team.

As I walked out of a crowd, Kumasi asked, "Ajamu, are you riding on the bus, or you riding with me and Tim in the box?" That's what Kumasi and I fondly called Tim's little square car: the box.

"Niglet, of course I'm ridin' with y'all. I just had to dap up a few of the homies first," I replied.

Tim chimed in, "Yohancé, you gotta focus, man. I get that you have a lot of friends tagging along with the robotics team to go on this field trip, but we can't keep losing you in crowds of people."

"Yeah, Ajamu. Focus," Kumasi said, piling on to Tim's words.

On our ride to the sports arena where the competition would be held, I thought Tim would be talking strategy and robotics. Instead, we spent most of the car ride talking about leadership and power.

"But what is the point of having any level of power or influence if you never use it, Tim?"

"Yohancé, the greatest complement to power is patience. When it *really* matters, that's when you act."

"Oh, I get it. So, if I ever get any real power, I should wait for the *really* beautiful women to come around before flexing."

"No, Yohancé. I'm saying you have to use that power just like that Air Force Major did to help us out a few months ago."

"Remind me what he did for us again, Tim? I barely remember him showing up to any of our meetings or being present at all."

"Yohancé, your principal didn't want to open up the school building on weekends just for us to be able to work on the robot."

"I remember that. Safety, security, and lawsuits, yada yada. Right?"

"That's correct," Tim said, "but Major Scissors made one phone call to his higher-ups and flexed his Air Force muscles. Remember how we never had an issue getting the school opened after that?"

"Yeah, I remember that. Tim, this whole United States Air Force Academy thing might be a good look," I said.

"Yeah, Yohancé. We just need you to become a General in the Air Force. That way Crenshaw High's robotics team never spends another weekend locked outside of the robotics room," Tim uttered triumphantly.

"I could become a General someday," I said as I surveyed the car full of my teammates. I was already their captain.

"Yup, but you have to watch what you do as a leader and not just what you say. You won't be a great leader, much less a General, if no one wants to listen to you," Tim warned.

"What? Tim, people listen to me. The boy listens to me," I said as I pointed at Kumasi in the backseat. "Ain't that right, niglet?"

"No," Kumasi said as he shook his head at my buffoonery.


**The Competition**

*FIRST* (For Inspiration and Recognition of Science and Technology) is the largest robotics competition in the world. Students and their mentors have teams ranging in size from three people to three hundred or more. The biggest teams, known as super teams, have a huge advantage. But they mostly use that advantage to help the smaller teams out. They are always willing to lend a helping hand or rebuild your whole robot if you ask them. The whole competition feels like one giant flea market, where everyone is trying to help one another prepare for their next match.

When the giant voice calls for the next match to begin, alliances are formed, and a three-on-three match ensues. The teams in the following match rush their robot from the pit to the match arena, gearing up for the chance to test their metal. If the schedule of matches has a team competing back to back, then this whole ordeal can become kind of hectic. But truly this is a chaos that one can get used to.

This would be Kumasi's first *FIRST* Robotics Competition, but a seasoned veteran like me already knew how this whole thing would go down. We were going to lose. Period.

So instead of stressing over every broken part of our robot after a lost match, or pulling my hair out over repeatedly failed re-inspections, I just said fuck it.

Here I was, the captain of a ship destined to sink, so I decided to enjoy the heck out of the journey. No one else knew that I'd come to the competition this year with this particular mindset, but they quickly figured me out.

"Yohancé, there you are! Why aren't you with the robot? Our match is up next," Tim bellowed at me. I promptly borrowed the tools I needed from these cute girls I was talking to, and returned to our robot.

**One hour later**

"Yohancé, where were you at during our last match? We took a beating and now we need you to fix the chassis and the claw elevator system. We've been looking for you for twenty minutes!"

"Tim, I'm on it. Let me just get this other girl's number, and I'll be right over there."

"No! Now, man. Now! Let's go," Tim said as he hustled me away.

**Another Hour Passes**

"Ajamu, I'm about to go drive the robot for our next match. Can you go talk to team 1515 (Beverly Hills High School) and make sure our autonomous modes are synced?" Kumasi asked.

Typically, captains talk to other captains when they need to coordinate, so this was my chance to talk to all the hot rich chicks from Beverly Hills. I was overly enthusiastic about my next job.


## One More Hour Passes

"Dude, where the fuck have you been?" Tim whispered through his boiling red frustration.

"Tim, I was with 1515 handling some business." At this point I was the only one smiling.

"Yohancé, you are not being a very good leader right now. Actually, you are being kinda shitty." Tim said this last part in the pit where more than a dozen of my classmates were watching us. Oblivious to the newly festering disdain for my antics, I decided to crack jokes instead of own up to my shortcomings.

"Tim, all the Skittles I'm used to are purple ones. But out here they got white girls, Latino girls, Asian chicks, and exotic mixed flavors. Tim, I'm tryna taste the rainbow."

"That's not funny, Yohancé. We need better from you."

"But what if I'm giving you guys my best? What if this is who I am?"

Tim Wright never answered my question. He just shrugged as I watched all the anger on his face turn to disappointment. His face was no longer red, it was pink, and his glasses seemed to slump down his nose in defeat. It was like watching Santa Claus on the verge of tears as he realizes you might belong on the naughty list.

For the rest of the competition, I tried to hold on to the modicum of respect that Tim, the other mentors, and the rest of my classmates had for me. I had to figure out what parts of my character that day were so negative and off-putting. Part of that negativity I wanted to keep, to remain authentic or *real*. But most of that stuff needed to go. It was part of a past that could only hold me back in my future.

# Chapter 33
# USAFA: Climbing a Mountain of Red Tape

IN EARLY AUGUST, just before the beginning of senior year in high school, most students start focusing on college applications. While I had started working on my applications almost a year in advance, I was still terribly behind my actual competition. I wrote one essay as a personal statement that I would send to all the colleges, and I thought I was ready to breeze through all of my applications. That is until I realized that applying to the United States Air Force Academy was nothing like applying to a regular college or university.

I compiled a list of about thirty or so schools I wanted to apply to, and later cut that list down to the twenty I could see myself attending. The first to go were schools that would not waive my application fee. If I couldn't afford to apply, then I certainly could not afford to attend.

My second round of cuts addressed personality and majors. If a school didn't strike me as the type of place that would build my character as well as hone my mind, I scrapped their application. When I got the number of eligible schools down to fifteen, I opened all applications at the same time. Each one seemed to need only a few mouse clicks for uploading documents. Some Ivy League schools wanted a little more information. But that was nothing compared to the United States Air Force Academy's throat punch of an application.

Getting through a USAFA application required an act of God. Unlike other applications, every step of the process was locked behind a time gate that could only be accessed by completing certain tasks first. Verification of citizenship, criminal background checks, authenticating birth certificates, and verifying social security numbers were all included in the first step of unlocking this Pandora's box of an application. When I received my pass-word to their website several weeks later, from a government agency, I thought the cryptic steps of their application process were over. They had just begun. My next task was to make contact with Major "Never Answers Phone"—no further instructions.

I spent two months calling Major "NAP" twice a day, until I finally got him on the phone. Most students contact this person on their application during their junior year rather than their senior year, so my urgency as a new candidate came as a surprise to the Major. He agreed to meet me at a local coffee shop to have our first interview. He arrived in his pilot's uniform, standing six-foot-two. He was a medium-build white guy, confidence shooting out of his pores. Diners gushed and thanked him for his service. He was a rock star. When he joined me at the table, I shook his hand and immediately started to analyze him. I had to figure out what button to push to make this man my ally.

"Yohonts, I … I am saying it correctly, right? Yohants?"

"No sir, but it's OK. I have more important things to discuss than how to pronounce my name."

"Yes, but let's start there first. I don't have a lot of time, and I would like this meeting to be fruitful."

He was not being hostile, but his tone revealed to me that he had already made up his mind about how this meeting would go. He questioned why I wanted to go to USAFA instead of any other college or university, and why I thought I was good enough. He was straight to the point, so I answered him succinctly. I told him my grade point average, a few of the courses I was taking, and my belief that USAFA was the best school to hone my mind and character.

The Major asked me whether I considered myself an athlete, so I answered with a rundown of my sports accolades. None of my answers seemed to impress him. Plus, he looked uncomfortable in his seat, as if he were ready to end the meeting. Then he asked me one last question.

"Yohancé, what does a typical day look like for you?"

"Sir, I wake up every day at three thirty and pull my little brother down from the bunk bed to let him know it's time to go. We get dressed and leave the homeless shelter so we can take public transportation to our high school. It takes about two hours to catch two buses and two trains to reach school. I take a schedule of honors and Advanced Placement courses. They're challenging, yet rewarding. After school, I belong to every club and team possible. I am currently captain of the robotics team, track team, chess club, and football team. I do not participate in any activities that have to do with going home after school, because I'm homeless; I do not have a home. I only have a place to push the reset button, and most nights I get too busy to find a decent amount of sleep."

Suddenly, the Major's whole demeanor changed. He stared at me in disbelief, and I let the awkward silence between us linger. I wanted the full breadth of my words to sink in.

He began telling me that between work in the Air Force, having a new child, and his new business that required him to travel around the world, he would be far too busy to give me the attention I needed to complete my application on time. Instead of letting my application fall through the cracks, he would recommend me to his bosses in the admissions office.

I was blown away. I wondered which detail in my speech had pushed him over the threshold and turned the Major into one of my biggest supporters.

After our meeting, I returned to my application to find all of my gates unlocked. I smiled like I had just won me a million dollars. I could finally see the whole application. Even though it was monstrously long and intrusive, being able to see the finish line gave me hope.

Many of the sections were time-intensive, or meeting- and interview-based, so I scrolled past these parts to find what I could complete right away. There was a section marked in red with lots of warnings on it, so I read it very closely, anticipating this to be one of the many trapdoors in the form. Answering wrong on this section looked like it could terminate my whole application, so after reading every detail, I selected my answer—Yes.

I had never felt dumber for telling the truth in my entire life. The question asked if the applicant had ever done any illegal drugs before. I checked the box that said yes. The red section of the application started extending past the length of my computer screen. As I scrolled down, I could see they required psychological evaluations and police reports. The whole document was now more than doubled in size, and it was still growing. I felt so angry at myself for having this stupid idea in my head that I must tell the truth. This thing called character had just cost me everything, and I was no better of a man for it. There was nothing left for me to do but stare at the ceiling and fight back tears of defeat.

How I would convince the United States Air Force to accept me with my drug history was beyond my comprehension. How could I convince them to give a half a million dollars' worth of education to someone with my past? Air Force officers and pilots had to be squeaky-clean, perfect. Why would they want someone like me?

Suddenly I knew it was possible. And easy. That's how I would present it to the Air Force. How many kids did they know who grew up homeless with their mother on Skid Row in Downtown Los Angeles? How many USAFA Graduates were once bouncing around shelters? So what if I did a few drugs? I quit all that by age eight. I had been clean for nine years now. I did things early. I had my first kiss before the first grade. I'd done more drugs than most teens before elementary school. Now, all I had to tell the Air Force was the truth. That way, they would get out of my way so I could continue my path.

I hopped back on the computer to continue scrolling through all my other tasks. I needed either the President of the United States, a United States Senator, or a Congressperson to interview me and recommend me to attend USAFA. Easy, next task.

I needed to write three separate personal statements and upload them in less than a week. Even easier, next task.

They wanted fitness tests, blood tests, eye tests, and a fleet of physicians to finally recommend me for service. Too easy, done.

No task seemed impossible to me. I had made up my mind that nothing would stop me from getting into the United States Air Force Academy.

The Major passed me on to his boss, Colonel Steve Stazo. It became evident to me that he was the only person on the planet whose determination to get me into USAFA matched my own.

"Yohancé, let me take something off of your plate. What part of the application can you use my help on?"

"Colonel Stazo, can you reach out to my local government official, or the POTUS? However much pull you have, sir. I need you to use it to get me a nomination to the Academy."

"Yohancé, you are not qualified to receive a presidential nomination. But you are allowed to accept any district nomination in the state of California, since you are homeless."

"Can you work on arranging any interviews or paperwork I need from these government officials, sir? You set it up, and I'll knock it out of the park, Colonel."

"I'll do that and more, Yohancé. You keep working on the application, and I am going to work on getting you a visit to the Hill."

"Yes, sir. Umm ... Colonel Stazo, what is the Hill?"

"Yohancé, that is what we call USAFA. It means a lot to Academy graduates, and I am sure they will explain it to you on your visit."

# Chapter 34
# Planted Every Seed I Could

PEOPLE HAVE OPENED so many doors of opportunity for me. If they ever call on me, I want to be ready to pay them back, because I owe all of my success to them. The C5 Youth Foundation called on me, and though I had a thousand excuses (college applications to complete, football practice to attend, AP Calculus homework), I had to answer their call.

The foundation took inner city kids from Los Angeles and brought them to Wyoming to learn to ride horseback, canoe, and camp. They instilled a sense of leadership in me.

**The Deed**

One day C5 said they really could use my help with a community-service project. Their plan was to clean up our local parks and plant trees. All that I had to do was show up to my old middle school, where a bus would take us to our different worksites. I was going to make South Central Los Angeles great again.

But it turned out that the bus drove to the Valley, where we were going to go clean up the parks. Unbeknownst to me, here was a community much more impoverished than ours. This area was full of gangs, crime, and homeless shelters that fought to reverse this negative cycle of poverty. I felt like I was being tricked, because I wanted to give back to *my* community.

Soon I realized that we were in *my* neighborhood. The *place* was only a few blocks away, and I had been to this exact park more times than I could count.

My old camp counselor, Mynor, was running the show. I took the tools from him and began working with a small team. I got into my pushy competitive mode again—even though this was charity work. I informed all of my old camp buddies that our small team would be doing more work than anyone else; we would be the only group to work through lunch that day. We were going to plant every damn tree we could, and not leave this park until every speck of trash was cleaned up.

When the day was over, our group boarded the charter bus to go back down to South Central. I tried to stay back, but Mynor would not let the bus leave without me. I had to confess to him that this was my hood—and that I lived in a nearby shelter.

"So that's why you were working so hard today, dude? I thought you were just trying to make up for all the times you didn't show up to our community service events."

Mynor understood. He thanked me and sent me off with extra sandwiches that were left over.

I thanked Mynor and waved at all my buddies on the bus as they left. I knew none of my buddies understood how important that day was for me, but I didn't need them to.

## Lauded by ESPN

G-Man is not a very nice person, but he is a kind man, if that makes any sense. I remember after stepping off the plane to Atlanta, Georgia, he told me, "I didn't fly you out here to accept no awards and look pretty on TV, YOH-HON-SAY."

The team was traveling across the country to put a hurting on North Gwinnett, who had challenged us for some reason. The game would be broadcast on ESPN, and only the best players at Crenshaw could go. It's not as if we could afford to fly the entire team across the country, so every seat in that airplane was filled by a Crenshaw Cougar that was ready to punish those Georgia boys.

It felt like everyone else got to enjoy their "little vacation" but me. G-Man kept me close to him and regulated everything I ate. He was trying to keep me from overindulging. The team got to go to these lavish buffets and eat all this great southern cooking, while G-Man and I ate vegetables. To be fair, he had been regulating my diet for quite some time. I had been having digestive issues from eating random food, and G-Man didn't like how my stomach was keeping me from playing at my best.

"Don't eat *anything* I don't give you, YOH-HON-SAY. I need you healthy for this game, hear?"

"Yes, G-Man. I understand."

I watched as my teammates gorged themselves on southern fried chicken, and I pined over their wasted scraps. I'd eat those if G-Man would let me, but I had to settle for the corn, peas, carrots, and fish that crowded my tiny plate. I wasn't ungrateful, though. G-Man was making sure I was fed, and I would return the favor by slamming a few people into the dirt later that week.

A few days before the game, G-Man had all of the players fill out biography sheets so the announcers could talk about them, to guarantee a more entertaining show. A couple of players were even getting awards. But when they heard about my community service, they said that I would be winning the biggest award of the night. When the game was about to start, I envisioned some grand presentation where I would accept my award on national television and give a speech.

But instead, G-Man pointed out the brief tribute that appeared on the TV screen. It was time for me to pay my end of the bargain, to do what G-Man flew me across the country to do. My five seconds of fame were over.


It bugged me that ESPN spent so little time highlighting the thing I actually cared about, community service, and focused on my sports record instead. Still, I had a really good game that day, and ESPN even did a slow-motion replay of me destroying a quarterback in an open field tackle.

Proof that I was in fact the Captain of the Chess Team.

# Chapter 35
# USAFA: Escorted to the Hill

I WAS TALKING to Dr. Ramsey, telling him with a thrill in my voice that the Air Force Academy was about to fly me to their school on an all-expenses-paid trip. I couldn't believe it. But Doc, who always had an understated response to my excitement, responded calmly.

"Mr. Salimu, this is what colleges do when they recruit athletes—and they usually offer a scholarship, too."

"Doc, you're not getting it. I'm not being recruited to play sports. I don't even think I'll play college sports."

"Yohancé, why not get a football scholarship to any one of these colleges? If you're good enough to get a scholarship, why not take it?"

"Dr. Ramsey, I don't want to attend college and have my peers think I only got in because I could run fast or throw a ball. I'm smart enough to make it into these schools on academics."

"Mr. Salimu, when did you start caring about what anybody else thinks about you?"

"Doc, I have always cared about that kind of stuff. There's usually just this huge wave of confidence that overtakes me and allows me to forget about it."

"I think I understand you, Mr. Salimu. Is there anything I can help you with as you prepare for this trip to the Air Force Academy?"

"Since you asked, there is something I could really use your help with, Doc."

"Yohancé, my gesture was more of a courtesy than an offer. You know, you lean on the kindness of others a little too much at times."

"I promise you, Doc … You are one of the few people I have ever let help me this much."

I explained that I needed to borrow a warm jacket or two, since the Academy was located in The Rocky Mountains of Colorado. I'd heard it was always snowing at that altitude.

Dr. Ramsey pushed back, asking why a boy from Southern California would choose college in such a terribly cold place. I had a good answer for him.

"Doc, I've already been through hell and back. I'm not going to let a couple of snowflakes stop me from grabbing what's already mine."

## The Zoo

From the outside, the United States Air Force Academy looked like a mystical grand citadel with lots of room for secrets. The long, winding, icy roads up the forested mountain made this military base perfect for hiding an amazing school that accepts only a privileged few. I felt like I must have cracked some special gaming code for them to invite me inside to observe their secret operations. I was here for three days to shadow a student, Cadet Martinus Davis, as he took part in his classes and activities. There were many tours and briefings as well, but my day always ended with Cadet Davis. My never-ending questions about USAFA kept him up late every night. Eventually he'd pass out from exhaustion, and I'd have nothing but my own thoughts to entertain myself in the dark. I'd lie awake in the dorm room, contemplating what further questions to ask cadet Davis when he woke up. I had a great one already planned when morning came..

"Cadet Davis, why do they call this place the Hill?"

"Yohancé, there are multiple layers to answering that question. It would be easier if I showed you something first."

Cadet Davis waited as I managed to get on all the layers of clothes that I needed. I was wearing four outfits at the same time, and was wrapped tightly in a long wool trench coat that Dr. Ramsey let me borrow. When we stepped outside of the dormitory building, a gust of disrespectful wind was blowing a pack of cadets across the Terrazzo. That was the name for twenty acres of a vast concrete jungle in the shape of a giant rectangle. In the center of the concrete rectangle was a seven-acre square grass field.

Thousands of men and women in uniform were scrambling into formation around the Terrazzo, as the winter gusts continued to push them across the marble and concrete floor. I watched the packs of cadets assemble into giant packs called squadrons, where they would shout commands and shift in unison. I had another thousand questions for Cadet Davis about what was happening. But when I turned to him, he was frozen in a rigid stance, his eyes trained intently on a small hill in the center of the Terrazzo.

A man in uniform started playing a bugle on the top of the hill, and I scrambled to mimic Davis's stance. I didn't want to be disrespectful of this ritual, even as an outsider. When the song was finished, the large squadrons marched one by one into a massive building they called Mitchell Hall. Now was my chance.

"Cadet Davis, what was that all about?"

"That's called Reveille, and we do formations and marching like that at least once a day."

"It looks really cool—and disciplined. Is that big mound in the center of the Terrazzo the Hill?"

"Yohancé, you can call this area the Teezo for short. And yes, that hill is sort of the Hill, but the full meaning is a bit deeper than that."

"You know, you guys have all this secretive jargon, Cadet Davis. What exactly do you guys mean by the Hill?"

Cadet Davis took a deep breath and laid out the story for me, by heart. He explained that another nickname for USAFA was the Zoo, because cadets are always on display. There were always VIP visitors to see them in action, from high-ranking military to Congress members—and even the President on occasion. They come to watch USAFA produce the best and smartest leaders in the country.

When people call this place the Hill, Davis continued, it's also a reference to the heightened sense of exposure cadets feel from the supervision of both superiors and visitors. But literally it also refers to the hill in the middle of the Teezo.

I listened with wide eyes and didn't interrupt him.

"There are a few traditions that we have at the school that reaffirm the reason we call this place 'the Hill.' But I can't tell ya much more than that. Some secrets are just for us to know."

I promised myself I would work hard enough to know their secrets one day.

We left the Teezo for Mitchell Hall, a massively tall building with ceilings so high that full-sized military planes were hanging from the rafters. Every wall was made of glass and presented a crystal-clear view of the snowy mountains in the background. I watched more than four thousand people march up between row after row of tables, and stand quietly still.

They had the same rigid frozen posture that cadet Davis had displayed earlier. All of them looked obediently at the Air Force General on the massive balcony before them.

"Take seats!" the General commanded in a booming voice.

All four thousand people quickly sat down, and every table was suddenly covered with breakfast food. This man was a wizard! He could feed thousands of people with two words, when I had barely been able to feed myself throughout my entire life. Whoever this man was, I was going to need everything he had, and I was ready to ask him how to obtain it. At the end of breakfast, we got to meet this general outside Mitchell Hall. He stood tall and addressed us.

"Good morning, students. My name is General Dick Clark, and I am the Commandant of Cadets at your United States Air Force Academy."

He was not the highest-ranking military official at the Zoo. But when it came to supervising cadets in the Cadet Wing, he was the head honcho. Period. Point blank. Full stop.

He shook each of our hands. As he came up to me, I looked in his face. He looked just like me, and it was eerie staring into what felt like a more mature reflection of myself. His arms were bigger than mine, though, and he looked like he could actually win in a fight against Mike Tyson, who we both resembled.

General Clark just smiled and told me, "The Air Force Academy tends to attract a certain type of person. Maybe you are the one who is supposed to fill my shoes when I retire from the Air Force."

**The Tour**

After our meet-and-greet with General Clark, we were introduced to the person responsible for our trip: Colonel Carolyn Benyshek, the Director of Admissions. Again, the students in my group acted like they were meeting a celebrity.

My tour group to USAFA was being hosted through the diversity recruiting program. Many candidates seemed to be a lot more like each other, and a lot less like me, which made me wonder what made them diverse. But I understood diversity to encompass a lot more than race or socioeconomic background.

Colonel Benyshek won my heart; she was a precise and professional women, with a sense of drive. After the stiff formality of the meet-and-greet, she relaxed. Colonel Benyshek explained the upcoming events and what we could expect—and what was expected of us as guests at USAFA.

When Cadet Davis took me to class, I got very excited. We were going to his Chemistry (Potions) class. It was a subject I'd always been very good at. As we descended through the academic building, I began to wonder if I was even smart enough to attend this school.

Chemistry class was nothing short of a blast. I found the instructor liked being questioned by his students. The instructor wanted us to calculate the energy in an exothermic reaction that would cause a bomb to save our allies on the ground by disabling the vehicles of our enemies. He was surprised at my proficiency in stoichiometry. I consistently was the first one to volunteer to come to the board. The cadets were surprised that I could follow the lesson. I knew that if the rest of the courses were anything like Chemistry class, then I would have no issue excelling academically at USAFA.

Our next event was a visit to the USAFA Preparatory School. This school was on the same massive military base as the college, but it had a slightly different structure. The students here were called cadet candidates, and they had to go to school and train for one year until they could be enrolled at USAFA as a cadet. Every new class at USAFA was only allowed to be roughly one thousand cadets, and the prep school usually took the first two hundred of those slots. There were also a dozen or so other preparatory schools around the country that would funnel candidates to USAFA, which effectively shrank the number of available slots for someone like me. Before my visit, I thought I was simply competing for one of the one thousand slots available each year. I was actually fighting a larger field of competition.

The official preparatory school that was on the base was much different than the other schools around the country. There was a much higher acceptance rate for the cadet candidates at the "P." A couple of the students even took most of their course load up on the Hill. The cadet candidates received an additional year of training and were compensated at a higher rate than the cadets on the Hill. While cadets received a monthly stipend of a few hundred dollars, cadet candidates received more than a thousand a month, and their year as a cadet candidate counted as a full year of active duty service.

I could see why these cadet candidates at the P thought they had a sweet gig, but I didn't think it was right for me. The P was designed to prepare students militarily, athletically, and academically to succeed as cadets on the Hill. I felt I was already prepared to go up there and kick some butt, so spending an extra year trying to get my degree felt wasteful. I wanted to reach the finish line as fast as possible.

## The Revelation

My last night at USAFA came too fast. I wasn't ready to go back to being that little homeless boy in South Central. I wanted to be a cadet. Cadets were never hungry. Cadets were never threatened by gang violence. Cadets had a warm bed every night. I was jealous of Cadet Davis and everything he had. I became emotional as I lay in the pitch-black dorm room.

"I wanna go to USAFA," I whispered into my pillow as warm tears began rolling down my face.

*You need to go to prep school first!*

It was my damned annoying inner voice. Again with bad news. I did not want to go to prep school, so I decided to challenge the voice.

"Why would I spend five years in college when I'm smart enough to graduate in four?"

I received no answer.

"Why would I accept one more obstacle to my path to success?"

I received no answer.

"Why should I listen to your bullshit advice?"

I received no answer.

I fell deeply into prayer to find some sort of answer, but nothing came. I was afraid that my tears and praying would bother Cadet Davis, so I buried myself deeper into my pillow. I stayed there sobbing for hours until it finally dawned on me. I had to figure out why I needed to go to the prep school, and how I was going to get there. My best answer was that I needed the money. Otherwise, Kumasi would suffer. I had become this pillar, supporting my family. The only way I could go to college and continue to be that pillar was to attend a college that was free and would also pay me a decent amount of money. The USAFA Preparatory School wasn't just my best option, it was my only option.

## Revectoring

Colonel Stazo picked me up at LAX and was driving me home. He seemed more enthusiastic than ever.

"So, how was your trip to USAFA, Yohancé? You do still want to attend the school after seeing what it's all really about, right?"

Breaking the news was going to be difficult. I took a deep breath.

"Sir, I think I want to go to the United States Air Force Academy Preparatory school first."

The colonel gripped the steering wheel of the car a bit tighter, but his face showed no sign of his frustration.

"But Yohancé, you have the grades and test scores to go directly into USAFA as a cadet. You know that, right?"

"Yes, Colonel Stazo, but I'd like to go to prep school first."

"Did you know that you can't apply directly to the prep school, Yohancé? I'm not sure I can get you in. Do you really need the extra year?"

I needed to convince Colonel Stazo that I needed this, but I couldn't figure out a way how. In the absence of a smart way of framing my argument, I told him my truth, or at least the part I was willing to share with him—I certainly wasn't about to tell him about my inner voice. I explained that my motivation was financial, and that the extra five to eight hundred dollars that the prep school cadet candidates get in their stipend every month would go a long way toward helping my family. If my little brother was not eating, I wouldn't be able to focus on my studies on the Hill.

Bullseye. I had used the correct combination of words, because Colonel Stazo's whole demeanor changed. He was confident he could sell my reason to the Admissions Department, and get me a slot at the prep school.

Then he switched topics to discuss jobs in the Air Force.

"Yohancé, have you heard of a UAV or RPA? The Air Force keeps changing the names of them, but basically I'm talking about the planes we fly remotely—drones."

"Yes, sir. The movie I watched where I first heard about the Air Force Academy had a few of them in it. I think the plane was called a Predator."

"Yeah, those are the exact kinds of planes I'm talking about, Yohancé. Do you think you would ever want to fly those?"

"They look cool sir, but I'm not sure what job I would want to do in the Air Force just yet."

"Just keep that job in mind, Yohancé. Those planes are the wave of the future, mark my words."

# Chapter 36
## G-Man Lays the Smackdown

ATTENDING CLASS AT the Shaw had never been boring to me, but after spending half a week at USAFA, I was restless to graduate. I could not stop fantasizing about my next school. Sitting in Mrs. Sidwell's Gifted Magnet Advanced Placement Calculus class just didn't do it for me anymore. I found I'd rather be a cadet than integrate tangents or find the derivative of a complex quadratic.

Mrs. Sidwell was twenty-six, a five-foot-seven blonde whose soft voice sounded like she should be singing in a Disney movie rather than teaching calculus. But she was a hard-ass when she needed to be. She noticed my daydreaming—and was not happy. Every time she saw my eyes glaze over, she would send me to the whiteboard to solve a problem. One time, as I was punished again with a whiteboard assignment, I happened to look to the side.

The doors to our classrooms had a small window in them, and peering at me through this glass frame was a familiar face. Greg Pope, a star on the football team, was laughing at me and waving a small piece of yellow paper. Noticing the distraction, Mrs. Sidwell rushed to the door and flung it open.

"Why are you outside my door distracting my students, Mr. Pope?"

Pope was scared by her response. He fumbled the yellow piece of paper, as he stammered, "Ma'am, I ... I have a summons for Yohancé. It's from G-Man."

Pope thought he'd said the magic words, because G-Man's name was a currency in and of itself through the halls of Crenshaw High.

"So what!" Mrs. Sidwell exclaimed, no longer sounding like a Disney princess. "My students do not leave this classroom, even if they receive a summons from the President himself! You will have to wait until my lesson is finished!"

Pope acted like the teacher had turned into a fire-breathing dragon, but in that moment I wanted to make a joke like, "Not even the Pope could take me out this class!" Miraculously, I held my tongue. Mrs. Sidwell was not in the mood to hear my smart-ass remarks.

Pope decided to give it another go and said, "Ma'am, if I don't come back with Yohancé, G-Man might ..."

"He's not leaving this classroom, so you better figure it out! The choice is yours—Cougar Pride." She used our school motto on him; teachers loved bouncing it off students to make a point. Pope made an effort to shrug off the scolding, but he had been crushed. Just as he walked away from the door, he looked me in the eye and pointed again at the yellow paper.

What did G-Man want from me that was so urgent? Why did he send Pope with a summons? I started to think about what I might have done wrong recently, because all I could picture was G-Man slapping the shit out of me. Our football season was going well, and even though we were not undefeated, we had destroyed nearly everyone he'd asked us to. My lockers were clean and not filled with smelly clothing, so what was the issue? Something was definitely wrong. But I wouldn't let it get me down as I marched to G-Man's office after calculus.

There were two guys laughing by G-Man's desk. But they were wearing team gear in different colors than our blue and gold. I looked at G-Man puzzled.

"Sit down, YOH-HON-SAY! Let these two recruiters holla at you real quick," G-Man said. He seemed downright happy. But he usually did not like college football recruiters. He'd call them poachers and chase them out of our practices. These men at G-Man's desk must have been the real deal.

"YOH-HON-SAY, I've been trying to find the right school for you for a long time, and I think I done finally did it. This is one of them Ivy League schools I know you wanna go to. Talk to the man."

These recruiters had waited in G-Man's office all day to meet me, but like one of my greatest mentors, I would not beat around the bush or be extra friendly with football recruiters.

"What majors do you offer at your school?"

"How comprehensive is your tuition assistance and scholarship program?"

"What more would I gain in attending your school, other than a college degree?"

These recruiters answered every single question, but none of their answers were good enough. I told them that I did not want to waste their time further. I would never attend their school, and I looked both men in the eyes and made sure they understood how serious I was.

Only later would I understand how disrespectful my actions were toward G-Man. He had prepared for this meeting, only to see me turn my nose up at a free education. I thought I was being like him: strong, determined, decisive. He and I had already discussed my college applications, but I would not let him get me a football scholarship to USAFA. I'd turned down his help one too many times now, and this last time was too blatantly disrespectful.

"Yohancé, I will see your ass at practice today, correct?"

"Yes, G-Man. I will be exactly where I am supposed to be."

"Good! I'll see you then, partna!"

When he called me "partna," a reference to Tupac or Snoop Dog, it really shook me. It suggested that something was about to go down. I told myself that I wasn't really afraid. *What doesn't kill you makes you stronger.*


## The Sweet Chin Music

Practice was supposed to be hard. After all, we were returning to the city championship, and there was no way we were going to lose. I'd finally gotten a good understanding of all the intricacies of football, and it only took me until the end of senior season to get there. I was now playing smarter. I would not just run full speed toward the ball. I thought I was really getting the hang of things. But during practice that afternoon, things were different. G-Man's criticisms were unending.

"Run it again! Yohancé keeps messing up the play! B-gap, Yohancé, B-gap! Get it right!"

I was standing exactly where I was supposed to, and challenging the right gap in the offensive line, but G-Man said it was not good enough. We ran the drills over and over again, until G-Man was finally through with me "sabotaging" his practice.

G-Man threw his clipboard on the ground, walked briskly onto the field, and grabbed me by the facemask of my helmet.

"Yohancé, are you going to stop messing up my practice!?"

I now understood why grabbing facemasks was a huge penalty in football. G-Man controlled my whole body with his firm grip on my facemask. He made me feel like a puppet with unforgiving strings; I wasn't even a real boy anymore.

"If you can't listen to my directions, what makes you think you will ever survive at the Air Force Academy?"

"G-Man, I …"

"Shut up! Everyone is doing up-downs on my whistle now!"

!!!——!!!

G-Man blew his whistle, and the whole team dropped face first onto the ground. We bounced off the turf and chattered our feet as we waited to hear the whistle again. Between every whistle blow, G-Man had more choice words for me.

!!!——!!!

"Yohancé, are you going to quit on this team because I'm too hard on you?"

"No, G-Man!"

"Yes, you will! You think you got life made now that this academy is sending you on all these fancy trips!"

!!!——!!!

"G-Man, I …"

"Shut up, Yohancé! Get your feet up higher! And hit the ground harder next time!"

He yelled louder. And I worked harder. And it still wasn't enough for G-Man.

!!!——!!!

"You 'ain't gon' hurt this field boy! Hit the ground harder!"

!!!——!!!

"Get up! Get up! Get off the ground faster than that!"

!!!——!!!

"You think the Air Force Academy is gon' let your lazy ass lay around like that?"

!!!——!!!

"You better rethink this whole academy thing if you cain't follow simple instructions, Yohancé!"

!!!——!!!

"Yes, sir!" I said.

"Yes, sir? Oh! You think you're already at the Academy, do you? I'm not a sir, Yohancé. I'm G-Man!"

G-Man kept the pressure on, wearing me down. Telling me I wasn't really a Crenshaw Cougar. Saying I didn't have what it takes to go to the Air Force Academy. Saying I should quit the team. And jabbing me with questions about whether I thought he was picking on me.

Of course he was picking on me, but I was certain there was a profound reason why. This ass whoopin' ain't had nothin' to do with no stinkin' college football recruiters. Bullying, harassing, abusing; none of these terms meant a fucking thing to me in that moment. This was my dad teaching me a lesson, and I'd rather die trying to learn it than show my dad he was raising a little bitch.

"Do you feel like you have to work twice as hard as everyone else, Yohancé?" G-Man shouted.

Suddenly, I felt like his message had broken through. I knew what he meant. And I knew exactly what he wanted to hear back.

"G-Man, I understand," I sputtered as I fought to catch my breath. "Because of the color of my skin, I will have to work twice as hard as everyone else at the Air Force Academy."

"Wrong! Everyone get on the goal line, now! We are going to run sprints until Yohancé turns on that big brain of his and figures this one out!"

Sprints would surely be easier than slamming my body on the floor doing up-downs, so I wondered why G-Man wanted to shift punishments.

We usually ran sprints at the end of practice anyway, which made me hopeful that we were just wrapping up for the night.

The team always ran in three distinct groups. The first, and fastest, group consisted of smaller skill players. The second group were the medium bunch, and the last group were the big guys. I usually ran with the big guys, but today G-Man made me run with the skill players. We would sprint for anywhere from five to forty yards at a time; every run was timed. If a group did not run fast enough, they had to repeat their run. Because I had to run with the smaller and fastest guys, we were doomed to have to repeat a few runs.

"Skill guys are up! That means you too, Yohancé! On my whistle!"

When G-Man's whistle blew, I flew down the field, determined to come in first place in a pack of more than twenty Cougars. In hindsight, beating all of these lightning-fast players was actually a really bad idea. I was only fast for a big man. If these guys wanted to, they could smoke me every time.

"De'Anthony! How did Yohancé beat you across the line!?"

G-Man looked about ready to lash out at a player, but he maintained control. He never did anything he did not intend to do. De'Anthony Thomas aka the Black Mamba was the top high school football recruit in the whole country. And if I ever came close to him in a foot race, it was not because I was as fast as him; It was because De'Anthony was jogging. G-Man remedied the situation by making the whole group repeat our run, because De'Anthony was jogging.

Now that everyone was running their absolute fastest, I could not keep up. I started to get more and more tired the longer we ran, and my body started to shut down. Normally I would not be the first person to fail in our timed runs, but with the exceptionally high bar set in this new group, failure was my only option.

"Get your lazy ass off the ground, Yohancé! Breathe in through your nose and out of your mouth. Now get on the line and run it again!"

I was launching my body across the finish line and barely making the group time, but standing back up after was becoming increasingly challenging. G-Man was quite literally running me into the ground.

"Twice as hard, huh? You figured out the answer yet, Yohancé?"

I couldn't even remember the question because we had been running for so long. Every one of my thoughts pertained to keeping air in my lungs and life in my body.

"I guess not then? Get back on the line, Yohancé!"

I was done. My body had quit on me, and I was lying flat on the turf.

"Get up, bro. We don't even get tired, so you gotta stop faking. Come on, I'll help you," said Marquis Thompson. He was the starting quarterback, and the real team captain of our football team. He lifted me off the ground and sprinted down the field holding me tight under his wing. We did not make it across the finish line in time, but I thought that the amazing moment when Marquis carried a lineman across the field would be enough to end practice. I was wrong.

"Men, I need one last lap around the field from all of you. If I see any of you slacking, we will keep running. If Yohancé comes in last, we will keep running. The choice is yours—Cougar Pride."

Half the team had already taken off for the lap around the gridiron, and I was frantically searching for whatever energy I had left to complete this run. I fell forward and caught myself with one leg, then the other. Soon enough, I had momentum and was running again. Many of the other players were all running with me. We were hunting De'Anthony as we sped up to catch the lightning fast Black Mamba. He did not slow down for us, but he waved us welcome as we sped up to meet him. The whole team stampeded around the field together as we circled to meet G-Man at the bench on the sideline. These benches had a phrase painted on them: "Go Hard or Go Home!" They reminded me that I did not have a choice. All I could do was "Go Hard."

As we came to a huddle around G-Man, the cool night air soothed our aching muscles. We were all on one knee, anxiously anticipating G-Man's words of wisdom for us. He always spoke slowly and methodically in these moments.

"Well, men, last game of the season coming up here. The city championship. The game for all the marbles. The head coach from that there Carson team likes to wear a suit. He's gonna come out there in his fancy blue suit and shake my hand with his chest stuck out like some sort of *professional.* I'll be wearing the same types of clothes I always wear. I ain't puttin' on no show for nobody. We're gunna go down there, kick their butts, and pick up our trophy. It's as simple as that. Now let's get together and say the Lord's Prayer and be done with practice. YOH-HON-SAY, lead us."

*"Our Father, Lord in heaven*
*Hollowed be thy name.*
*Thy Kingdom come, thy will be done*
*On earth, as is in heaven.*
*Give us this day, our daily bread*
*And forgive us our trespasses*
*As we forgive those who trespass against us.*
*Lead us not into temptation*
*But deliver us from evil.*
*For God is the kingdom,*
*The power, the glory*
*Forever and ever*
*Amen."*

When we were done, I felt more pride in my team than ever before. We had survived one of the hardest practices, and we did it together. But I couldn't just let G-Man walk away. I had to know what he was trying to tell me on the field that day.

"G-Man, why was my answer not correct? I thought black people in certain situations, and minorities in general, had to work harder to attain certain levels of success."

"So, you still don't get it, do you, YOH-HON-SAY?"

"No, G-Man. I'm not always as smart as I think I am, and sometimes I just don't know the answer."

"Yohancé, that phrase does not apply to you at all. I've known your family for years, and I know your challenges. *You* need to work a thousand times harder than everyone else—and then ya only get half of what they got. If you don't bring your all to the Air Force Academy, you will not make it. Even if I didn't tell you this, you would eventually figure it out, though, 'cause you're a pretty smart kid, Yohancé. And in case for some reason you feel you need to hear these words, I'm proud of you."

# Chapter 37
# Meet Triumph and Disaster and
# Treat Those Two Imposters
# Just the Same

AS I HAVE said before, my favorite poem is "If," by Rudyard Kipling. This poem has been my biggest mantra ever since I memorized it in the eighth grade. It offers a set of instructions to becoming a man. One part in the second stanza really became my guiding philosophy:

> *If you can meet with Triumph and Disaster*
> *And treat those two impostors just the same;*

## Disaster

In the spring, most colleges and universities send out acceptance letters to prospective freshmen. At the Shaw, this time period is very exciting.

The Gifted Magnet students of my year all met in Mrs. Sidwell's Calculus class to share what schools we had been accepted to. A few classmates were accepted to prestigious schools: UCLA, Cal Berkeley, MIT, and UC Santa Barbara. I wanted to congratulate all of them. Instead, here's what I found myself saying: "Yeah, but I got into the Air Force Academy, so I'm still better than all of you."

I felt deeply embarrassed the second the arrogant words came out of my mouth. But instead of shutting my mouth, I piled it on thicker. I proceeded to pull out my phone and search for a few select emails I'd received several months ago. I was going to show my classmates all of the deans of various colleges and universities who had sent me personal emails guaranteeing me a full scholarship. But before I could be a bigger asshole, my legs carried me out of that classroom.

There were a few minutes before the lunch bell, so I headed to the cafeteria. My plate of food that day was all free breakfast food: eggs, grits, French muffins, cereal, and pancakes. My Styrofoam tray was loaded.

I left the lunch line in much better spirits than I'd entered it.

At that moment, I remembered that I had not yet talked to Rodney about what school he would be attending. More than anyone else in the Gifted Magnet program, I wanted him to succeed. But hanging with Rodney meant seeing members of the Calculus class that I had just insulted. Before seeing those guys, I had to check my ego. I understood what I had done wrong during class. I looked down at my huge tray of food and wondered whether it would attract attention and seem boastful. But I dismissed the idea and headed over to see Rodney.

"Damn that's a huge plate, Yohancé!" were the first words from my friend.

"Thanks, Rodney, I worked hard for it," I joked as I balanced the fragile Styrofoam tray.

"So … Air Force Academy, right? That was your number one choice, wasn't it?"

"Yeah, dude. It was. I'm actually going to attend their prep school for the first year, though."

"Is that still USAFA?"

"Rodney, I promise you, everything worked out perfectly for me. What school are you going to end up at?"

"Dude, I'm going to USC."

Rodney's good news about the University of Southern California put me into an exceptionally happy place. I looked around the quad, this large grassy area in the center of the school, and just took in the beauty of it all.

Just then, Tahj Walker strolled up. He was a friend in the Gifted Magnet Program, but also this huge practical joker. When he came up to Rodney and me, he gave me a smirk of disapproval.

"You think you're better than us with all that nasty-ass cafeteria food?"

As Tahj finished his taunt, he gestured in an upward motion toward my tray. Maybe it was an accident. Maybe not. Suddenly, the Styrofoam tray shattered and my lunch was covering my face and torso.

As I balled up my fist, preparing to strike him down, Tahj started apologizing profusely. My anger had turned me into a monster, and I contemplated how much pain I was going to inflict on this kid. Nothing mattered at that moment except revenge. But Kipling suddenly echoed in my head:

*If you can meet with Triumph and Disaster*
*And treat those two impostors just the same;*

I dropped my fist to my side, spun around, and walked briskly away from Tahj. I needed to leave as soon as possible, because my anger was still trying to push me over the edge. That stanza of Kipling's poem is about maintaining balance, and I was too close to my tipping point. I was ready to throw away everything and become that hard-ass nigga at the core of my existence. I fantasized about breaking Tahj's limbs, slamming him on the ground, and stealing his lunch money. But that wasn't me. That's who I could have become.

Learning to Tame My Anger

**Triumph**

When no one was looking, I beat my chest with one fist as I walked away from Tahj. It wasn't because I was proud of myself, though. It was because I was pretending to be a man. I was going to be tough and not let these emotions overwhelm me. I had no clue where I was walking, but my feet continued to carry me past crowds of people.

"Hey Yohancé, way to go in that city championship, man. I know it was a while back, but you guys kicked some butt for the Shaw!"

"Thanks, man. I appreciate that."

---

(HTTP://WWW.LATIMES.COM/)

# Football: Defense scores again for Crenshaw

DECEMBER 11, 2010 | 3:12 PM

**Yohance Salimu's** blocked punt that went out of the end zone for a safety has given Crenshaw an 18-0 lead over Carson with 1:17 left in the third quarter.

The big surprise of this City title game is the lack of offense from Crenshaw, which scored 44, 49 and 63 points in its three earlier playoff games.

**De'Anthony Thomas** had 46-yard run in the third quarter, and the Cougars switched to last year's quarterback, **Marquis Thompson**, in the second half, but their offense still hasn't produced any points.

The bad news for Carson is that Crenshaw's defense has bottled up quarterback **Justin Alo** from the start. He has been sacked twice but pressured many times. Both Crenshaw touchdowns came on interception returns in the first quarter.

Hurting both offenses have been illegal procedure penalties.

-- Eric Sondheimer

---

Lauded by The LA Times

I didn't know that kid's name, but I always liked getting praise from my peers. The brief conversation with him got me a bit turned around, and I found myself at the men's basketball gym. "This must be where I'm supposed to go," I murmured to myself.

When I opened the door, I saw one of my football coaches speaking to a group of students who were sitting in the bleachers. Behind them was a sign with three large letters on it: FCA. Coach Elimimian was wearing a shirt that read "Fellowship of Christian Athletes," and he invited me to come into their meeting. Coach E. introduced me to the group of underclassmen, but they giggled shyly and said they knew who I was already. I was flattered but played it cool.

After Coach E. prayed with the group, we broke into smaller groups to talk about our lives and pray for one another. Coach joined my small group, and we listened to each student's requests for prayer. I was not sure how much I was going to share with this group. When it was my turn to speak, I froze for a brief moment.

"Can you guys just pray that I get to eat dinner every night?" I started, and shock registered on every face. "I know it sounds weird, but I'm not guaranteed a meal every day, and fighting for every crumb I get is very tiresome." Coach E. looked at me in disbelief but then shifted back to general prayers. His shock proved to me that G-Man could keep a secret.

When the school bell rang, all of the kids dashed out of the gymnasium. As I held the door open for Coach E., he handed me a small cardboard box.

"Here, Yohancé. I know you came late and didn't get any pizza, so this whole box is yours."

It was just me and Coach E. standing in that doorway. As I grabbed the box, I almost shed a tear. I wanted to hug him, and maybe allow myself to break down right on the spot. But I settled for just two words.

"Thank you."

And just like that, triumph followed disaster.

# Chapter 38
# On Par with the Greatest

SOMEHOW, THEY'D PACKED all three hundred Crenshaw students from the graduating class of 2011 into an auditorium in the middle of the city. Most students sat shoulder to shoulder, tightly packed on what little floor space remained in front of the tremendous black stage. The Shaw seldom graduated this many seniors in one year; it was a cause for celebration.

A few lucky students sat on the stage and enjoyed bountiful leg room. Rodney and I were among them, because we were among the top graduates. I knew so little about these graduation ceremonies that I even had to ask him why our robes had a different gold trim to them. Everyone else only got to wear one of our school colors: royal blue. Folks on stage had a combination of royal blue with lots of fancy gold trimmings.

I didn't really care much for the ceremony; I just wanted to get my diploma and head off to USAFA. My mind was already in college as my friends bickered back and forth about the details of the proceedings. Apparently no one knew who our key speaker was. But who cares about stuff like that?

## Daydreaming Through Graduation
I never really thought about what I would be giving up going to a school like USAFA—a military academy—instead of a big-name school like UCLA. I had spent some time on both campuses, so what made them so different?

The resounding answer I came up with was *A Lot*. But mostly I wondered if name recognition of a school really mattered. USAFA is pretty well known, but everyone knows everything about the University of Crenshaw in Los Angeles. Or at least they think they do.

I remember during my summer attending classes at UCLA, I got into an argument with one of my teacher's assistants, Olaleke Owalabi. We called him Ola for short. I told Ola that I could not dunk a basketball because I was too heavy; my muscles held me down. Ola was a tall, skinny Nigerian man, and told me I was a fool to believe such nonsense. He insisted that he could teach me how to dunk a basketball just as easy as he'd taught me how to program in our robotics course.

I met Ola later that day at the UCLA basketball gym. He was standing in front of a huge display of trophies and pictures. I waited for him to finish reading a few of the captions before I greeted him.

"Hola, Ola. What are you reading?"

"Hello, Yohancé. You know your greeting is not very original, right? Everyone greets me in Spanish."

"It's probably because it's one of those jokes that never gets old, Ola."

"If you say so. Do you know who this guy is?"

"Yeah, I do. That's Kareem Abdul-Jabbar. He's the guy you pick when you want to cheat and just dominate everybody in whatever basketball video game you're playing."

Ola never laughed at any of my jokes. He just raised his eyebrow and asked his next question.

"OK. Well, what professional basketball team did he play for?"

"That's easy. All the best basketball players—past, present and future—play for the Lakers. So my guess would be that he played for the Lakers."

"That sounds like a lucky guess to me, Yohancé."

"Ola, I've been makin' lucky guesses my whole life. How do you think I made it this far?"

"Yohancé, you really don't know how great this man was at basketball, do you?"

"Nope. But I get the feeling you are about to explain it to me."

Ola shook his head at me in disappointment. How was he going to teach me how to dunk if I did not know who Kareem Abdul-Jabbar was?

"OK, Yohancé. Imagine this: You are so good at your sport in college, that they change the rules for everyone just to slow *you* down."

"I don't quite get it, Ola."

"Yohancé, imagine you were a boxer in college and you were so good at throwing a right hook, that no college boxer could throw that punch anymore. The punch was now illegal for everyone, and you could no longer use it to score points."

"Ola, that sounds crazy and highly exaggerated. What are you getting at here?"

"Yohancé, Kareem Abdul-Jabbar was so good at slam-dunking on people that all of college basketball made the move illegal. The whole rule was created to stop Kareem from dominating."

"That sounds … amazing. But I'm pretty sure players are allowed to dunk in college basketball."

"They took the rule away after Kareem graduated—true story."

"I'm sure you wouldn't lie to me about something like that, Ola, but I'm just a skeptical person. I gotta look it up for myself."

"Yohancé, the plaque documenting it is right there in your face!"

I stared—dumbfounded—at the plaque that said everything Ola had just told me. Apparently, Kareem Abdul-Jabbar graduated from UCLA— who knew?

## Lupe Fiasco—The Show Goes On

Rodney shook me out of my daydream like he had just seen a ghost. He was pointing in the direction where a giant was making his way to the stage. I couldn't believe my eyes. It was Kareem—motha-fuckin'—Abdul—motha-fuckin'—Jabbar. You can't say shit like that out loud. But I was definitely thinking it.

Kareem's speech was about elevation, progress, and continued success—values this seven-foot-two hall-of-famer epitomized. This sky-scraper of a man knew a thing or two about not resting on the laurels of one's past successes. He had been the most successful college basketball player in history, and he topped that off by becoming the best professional basketball player of all time. Now he was trying his hand at philanthropy by giving back to communities like mine.

"This is not your finish line," he told us. "Every one of you will have greater and greater successes. I want you to know that I believe in you, and in your continued desire to challenge yourselves in whatever way that may be."

Kareem's profound speech resonated with me so much that it was one of the few details of that ceremony that I remember vividly. As my classmates danced and backflipped across the stage to grab their diplomas, all I could think about was how I could do it. One day I could be just as great as Kareem Abdul-Jabbar. Maybe not at basketball, but I could definitely be on par with the greatest.

# Epilogue

Dear Reader,

You got to the end of the book! Or maybe you just skipped your way here. Regardless of how you did it, I want to thank you for reading my story. It took a lot for me to finally share it in deep detail. I got bored of investing so much time in playing video games and watching movies, so I finally decided to use my free time to write my memoir. I wrote the first draft in less than a month. But I was inspired in a much different way than most authors.

In July of 2019 I was stationed at Beale Air Force Base in California. I was feeling very down and depressed, so I spent four hours alone in my house, just praying and daydreaming and praying and daydreaming. God revealed himself to me that day and showed me why I was going through so much turmoil in my life. He gave me a front row seat to my own presentation. I watched myself tell the grand story of my life in front of thousands of people. When the *me* onstage was done, God handed me my book. He allowed me to flip through the chapters and see what I was going to write. The most important thing my vision showed me was why people would care to read my story. I met many of my fans that day, as I shook their hands and learned what a tremendous influence my story had on their lives. The events of my life in the book had already taken place, so I just needed to fill out all the chapters in the table of contents that God had shown me.

When I first started writing, I had a goal of writing only one book. It turned out that the book was far too long, and that my story was actually supposed to be told in three distinct books. The first book is about me at Crenshaw High; the second, me at the Air Force Academy; and the final book is about my professional career afterwards.

At the time of my writing this epilogue, I'm not sure how long it will take me to write the last two books, or if I will finish.

I wrote this whole first book from my bed, clutching my heart in pain, in disbelief of how close to death I was/am. I have two very rare heart conditions, but I'm super-confident that God only wants to slow me down in order to write this story with some real detail to it. If you liked my story and want to watch it unfold further, please be on the lookout for my other two books.

If you didn't like my story, you can kick rocks—I didn't write it for you. The rest of you, I have a lot of love for. I hope you spread my story so that it can influence more and more people. Thanks again, and see you at USAFA!

Sincerely,
Yohancé Salimu

P.S. Even though my story is completely factual, a memoir is about how I remembered my past. I get the last word. People who know me may remember different versions of these stories. That's cool; I invite them all to write their own book! When I was planning this book, I remember a conversation I had with my football coach.

"G-Man, I'm gonna write a book this year and tell the story of how you turned me into a man."

I remember the double take he gave me.

"Don't tell these folks no lies about me, YOH-HON-SAY. Might have to sue the pants off you."

"G-Man," I pushed back with a big grin, "if anything, I'll have to water the story down in order for people to believe it. And I hope you do sue me so I can finally pay you back for what you did for me."

P.P.S. My robotics team went on to establish a strong working relationship with the Aerospace Corporation. At least five people on my robotics team got jobs there after I was hired. One of those individuals was my little brother Kumasi, who, after graduating from Tuskegee University with his degree in physics, now works at the Aerospace Corporation full-time.

# Acknowledgments

First and foremost, I would like to acknowledge Deez Nuts. Deez Nuts got me through a lot. When I told my Uncle Tony about a few chapters in my manuscript, and what made my story different, he told me, "Boy, you got the biggest balls I done ever heard of!"

Damn straight I do.

Second, I wanna thank God and everyone he put in the village that raised me. I don't just mean the Baldwin Village (the Jungles). I am talking about every person who either directly or indirectly influenced my story at any and all turns.

Thank you, Rachel, because even though you almost killed me, you turned me into exactly the weapon God intended me to be.

Finally, I would like to thank my proofreaders, editors, publisher, and my whole damn literary team. You know who you are. And you know you're THE SHIT.

# About the Author

Yohancé Ajamu Ebu Salimu (Dadoom Da Doom Doom) is a fighter, a survivor, and a winner. Salimu graduated from Crenshaw Senior High School in California and went on to study Geospatial Science at the United States Air Force Academy (USAFA) in Colorado Springs, Colorado. Upon completion of his training and earning his degree in 2016, Salimu was commissioned as an officer into the Air Force as a part of the fifty-eighth graduating class of USAFA. Salimu progressed into piloting Remotely Piloted Aircraft such as the RQ-4 Global Hawk, as well as the MQ-9 Reaper. After completion of his service to his country, Salimu may have taken off the uniform, but he has never ceased in his efforts to serve others. He is now a highly sought-after public speaker, as well as the President and CEO of the nonprofit scientific research organization Geospatial Q & A Inc. The corporation bolsters economic and social growth in small communities utilizing applied research.

# Final Word

I am the President and CEO of Geospatial Q & A Inc.

- I do not pay myself a salary.

- I will use my story, this book, the speeches, and all the millions of dollars I generate to create opportunities for underprivileged youth (and I know exactly how).

- I will run the most efficient charitable organization ever!

- I did not write this story to make a quick buck! I wrote it because I will become the change I wish to see. I am tired of waiting on everyone else.

- I WILL LEAD!